PRIESTS AND WARRIORS

Social Structures for Cherokee Politics
in the 18th Century

AMERICAN ANTHROPOLOGIST

PRIESTS AND WARRIORS
Social Structures for Cherokee Politics
in the 18th Century

by

FRED GEARING

Memoir 93

THE AMERICAN ANTHROPOLOGICAL ASSOCIATION

Vol. 64, No. 5, Part 2, October, 1962

The AMERICAN ANTHROPOLOGIST is published six times a year in the months of February, April, June, August, October, and December by the American Anthropological Association. Subscription is by membership in the Association, which includes the issues of the AMERICAN ANTHROPOLOGIST and the MEMOIRS as published. Printed by George Banta Company, Inc., Menasha, Wisconsin. Second class postage paid at Menasha, Wisconsin. Accorded the special rate of postage provided for in paragraph 4, section 538, P. L. & R. authorized August 22, 1922.

Printing Statement:

Due to the very old age and scarcity of this book, many of the pages may be hard to read due to the blurring of the original text, possible missing pages, missing text and other issues beyond our control.

Because this is such an important and rare work, we believe it is best to reproduce this book regardless of its original condition.

Thank you for your understanding.

To

ROBERT REDFIELD

who said:

"We do not enact a science: It grows."

and other things echoed in these pages.

Acknowledgments

M Y DEBTS to the following persons are very large, and each debt seems to me incommensurate with the rest.

Fred Eggan planted in my student mind ideas which came to awareness by delayed action; he was not forewarned that I announce myself here as a structuralist.

Marjorie Gearing, my wife, graciously suffered the usual neglect. Through this and in many other ways, she gave me that measure of peace of mind which the work requires and which one enjoys.

Robert Redfield, to whom the book is dedicated, can be found on most pages: his affection for the tradition of anthropological inquiry, his special affection for those forms of anthropological thought which attempt to grasp the whole. And in these pages, certain primitive worlds move through some aspects of their transformations, coping, as Redfield knew men always do, with moral imperatives and imponderables.

Sol Tax early made it impossible for me to think of men as automatons. The Cherokees in these pages (though they are usually invisible as particular men) are sentient beings, creators as much as creatures of culture, and social structure is here something in the awareness of actors, under continuing, conscious, purposeful modification.

Robert Thomas, then fellow student, pressed me toward an understanding of Indians, Cherokees and others; his help permitted me to dredge meaning from very imperfect records, and he gave generously of his unusual fund of Cherokee knowledge.

This study, in its first form, was my dissertation at the Department of Anthropology, University of Chicago, so to that department, staff and student, I owe the additional debt for teaching me that much of anthropology which I was capable of learning and for giving me several most enjoyable years.

A grant from the Graduate School of the University of Washington allowed me free time, in the summer of 1959, to bring this work toward its present state. Further study occurred in the context of stimulating work with faculty and graduate students of the Department of Anthropology of the University of Washington in a program of training for research in non-Western political systems, begun the fall of 1959, which program also financed the preparation of the manuscript.

The index was prepared with dispatch and good judgment by Steven Piker, graduate student in anthropology at the University of Washington. The illustrations were done by Mrs. Cecilia Corr. Miss Charlotte Quigley was very helpful in the course of typing the manuscript. Final editing was done in the midst of a field trip.

FRED GEARING

Kardamili, Messinias
Greece
March, 1962

Table of Contents

List of Figures

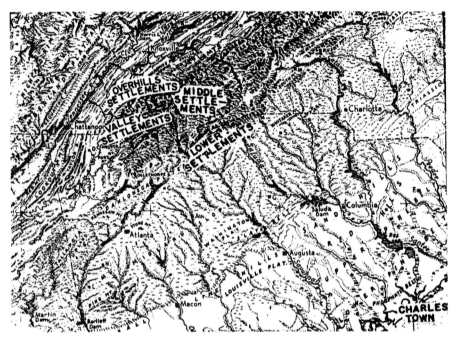

FIG. 1. A schematic map of Cherokee settlement (from Gilbert 1943, superimposed on a detail from *Landforms of the United States*, by Erwin Raisz, 1957).

Introduction

THE GREAT SMOKY MOUNTAINS run northeast to southwest. Two river systems rush out of the mountains, one eastward to the Atlantic Ocean, and the other west (then north) to the Ohio River, cutting deep V-shaped valleys. In the 18th century, Cherokee country lay across the range at right angles.

The rugged terrain partially isolated Cherokees from one another. Cherokees in one region fought Creeks and traded with South Carolina, while Cherokees in another fought Shawnees and traded with Virginia. Because of the isolation and out of such diverging regional interests, a sense of regional identification arose in four Cherokee sections. On the eastern mountain slopes, strung along the streams of the upper reaches of the Savannah river system, were the settlements of the Lower Cherokees. Here the land is rolling plateau out of which rise isolated peaks and through which rejuvenated streams cut valleys 50 to 150 feet deep. From these Lower settlements war trails led south to the Creek tribes, and other trails led southeast to Charlestown of the new colony of South Carolina. On the opposite slopes of the mountains, 100 miles northwest, were the Overhill settlements. Through this section of rolling country the Tennessee River and its tributaries drain westward, cutting valleys as deep as 500 feet; in these deep valleys the Overhill Cherokees had their settlements. From the Overhills, trails led west and north to the Shawnees, and other trails led north and east through the mountains to Virginia. The Lower and Overhill settlements were areas of much going and coming—exposed to alien tribes and first to meet competing Europeans who moved from the seaboard to trade, to plow new lands, or sometimes to fight. Between these two sections, partially insulated from the outside in tortuous mountain terrain, were the Middle and Valley settlements, tucked into the very narrow valleys of the upper streams of the Tennessee and Hiwassee river systems.

This semi-isolation among the four Cherokee sections was of sufficient age to permit regional dialects to form. Elati, now extinct, was the dialect of the Lower settlements; the Overhill and Valley settlements spoke Atali, now spoken in Oklahoma; the Middle settlements spoke Kituhwa, now spoken among the Cherokees of North Carolina (Gilbert 1943:199).

Between 10,000 and 20,000 Cherokees lived along the rivers in the early 1700's. Settlements were formed wherever the valleys provided sufficient flat land for gardens. These settlements ranged in size from two or three households to populations over 500; there were some 60 settlements, not counting the very smallest.[1]

In these settlements Cherokees built their homes, "square houses of poles or logs often containing three rooms and built one or two stories high . . . plastered inside and out with grass-tempered clay and . . . roofed with chestnut-tree bark or long broad shingles." Inside, the beds were boards covered with bear

1

skins; there was an open fire, utensils, and little else. Near each house stood a sweathouse, used by the ill to purify themselves (Gilbert 1943:316).

Many households included several nuclear families, related to one another through the women: a grandmother and her husband, one or several of her daughters and their husbands, and the grandchildren; to these might be added an adult male (son or grandson to the old woman) who was unmarried or had recently divorced and returned home. Some households contained only a husband and wife and their children.

To Cherokee mothers, daughters, and grandmothers each day, winter or summer, was much like the next—well filled with the incessant and various demands of daily household work. Every day, women and girls prepared food: corn, potatoes, beans, peas, melons, cabbages, and pumpkins from the gardens, and meat and fish brought in by the men. When they found time, the women made clothes from deer and buffalo hides, and from trade cloth. They made pots, wove baskets, and tended the sick. There were usually several babies, one's sisters' babies if not one's own, to be fed or comforted.

This daily rhythm of women's work was not much altered as the seasons came and went. In the summer there were gardens to be tended, but one did not stop cooking meals or caring for the sick; babies were wrapped up in winter and left naked in summer, but they had to be fed and comforted the same way all year. The activities of the men varied with the seasons, but their activities did not much affect the women's work. The young men were often absent in winter; in summer the women could watch them play lacrosse; there was a seasonal round of ceremonies run by the men. But the seasonal coming and going of the men and their affairs was but an environment, a backdrop against which the women went about their daily work.

Beyond this daily cadence, the women knew intimately a much larger rhythm, the coming of the new generations. Giving birth to sons and daughters, raising them, and helping one's daughters in turn give birth and raise their daughters, this was the essential meaning of female Cherokee life. To enjoy this larger rhythm was the hope of Cherokee women, and this larger rhythm made meaningful the daily drudgery.

The essentials of Cherokee life were bound up in those two rhythms of female work. If an adequate description of Cherokee life is ever drawn, the most crucial task of that description will be to depict those two rhythms. To feed and care for the household, and to bring along the next generation, these seem to be the only human tasks necessary for survival, and, for the Cherokees as for most human societies, these were done almost wholly by the women.

This study turns, however, to less important facts, to 18th century male life. Almost all of this less crucial male work unfolded with the seasons: an annual cycle provided the rhythm of life for Cherokee men. In late summer, the men helped with the harvest, then busied themselves for several weeks, under the leadership of the older men, with a series of three ceremonies and with councils. Through the fall and winter the young men hunted and warred, and in December there was another major ceremony. In the spring there was another ceremony, following which the men helped plant. In the summer, the young men played lacrosse against other settlements, occasionally hunted, and probably built or repaired public buildings, especially the large, seven-sided roofed structures which often held 500 during the ceremonies and councils; and at mid-summer there was a final major ceremony. Occasionally, without regard to season, it was necessary to revenge a murder or to exert pressures to prevent a wrongful marriage. Such was the work of the men.

This study considers, more particularly, that part of the work of Cherokee men which was political: decision-making by villages as single organized wholes, decision-making somewhat later by the new Cherokee tribal state, and the implementation of those group decisions.

The Cherokee political systems seem to have included two aspects. First, they consisted of personnel and procedures which helped villagers decide how to resolve conflicting interests regarded as impinging on the general welfare. Second, these political systems consisted of personnel and procedures for implementing those public policy decisions. These two aspects form the primary focus of this study, though other aspects will enter.

Since I set out to study Cherokee political life, I must deal with villages, not with Cherokee settlements. The village, as the term is used here, was a Cherokee political construct, formed of one or a few settlements. Settlements were often very small, but Cherokee villages could not have numbered much less than 350 individuals, because a smaller number could not have supplied sufficient old men to fill crucial village offices. Cherokee villages seem also to have hived off when populations reached upward toward 600. A village, then, is 350 to 600 souls, organized politically. In the early 1700's there were more than 60 settlements of various sizes; these appear to have been organized into some 30 to 40 political villages.

In order to describe village social machinery for politics, I shall imagine, throughout this study, a village of 400 souls, letting it stand for each of the 30 or 40 real Cherokee villages.

In the 18th century, Cherokee political activity unfolded in the midst of religious ritual. Each year, at noon on an appointed day in late September, when the kernels of the corn had become full and hardened, hence ready for harvest, the men of each Cherokee village gathered for a harvest ceremony. In each village, Cherokees carried green boughs and paraded before the village priest chief and his attendants outside the village council house. For four days they danced; at night the women joined them for social dances. After a lapse of a few days, with the new moon, Cherokee villagers celebrated the coming of their new year with a second ritual. At dawn, men, women, and children went into the village council house and made offerings before the perpetual fire. Then the village priest chief led the people to the river, full of falling leaves and therefore strong with medicinal powers at this time, and all bathed seven times. Then the village feasted. About ten days later, as decided by the priest chief, there followed still a third ceremony, perhaps the most vital. This ritual was explicitly devoted to the elimination of bad feeling among villagers, considered by

Cherokees as ritual impurity. The perpetual fire in the council house was ceremonially rekindled, the fires in every home were swept out, and from the sacred perpetual fire new fires were lit. People bathed in the river, letting their old clothes float downstream and putting on new clothes as they emerged. For four days village unity was ritually renewed and symbolically expressed, and by that very renewal and expression village unity was made in some large measure real.[2]

These three ceremonies, which occurred within a month or very little more, were one half of the annual major Cherokee ceremonies. The concentration of ritual events in these few weeks was not an accident of history, for during those same weeks the Cherokee villages were occupied also with a second, more difficult task. Each year during these weeks, interspersed among the three ceremonies, Cherokees held their most important village councils.

Cherokees approached that annual political task with what might be considered a self-imposed handicap. James Adair (1775:428), a trader among the Cherokees and other southeastern groups from 1735 on, wrote that chiefs could not command but only persuade, and that they did so by "good-nature and clear reasoning, or colouring things. . . . " Similarly, George Millingen Johnson, a surgeon active during a war with the Cherokees in 1761, wrote, "Subjection is what they are unacquainted with . . . , there being no such thing as coercive Power among them" (Milling 1951:185–86). These observations reflect certain Cherokee ideas about decent conduct; as applied to the operation of village councils, they meant that no council decision could be reached until there was unanimity.

On many of the days between the ceremonies there were formal council sessions. A white standard was raised, and the whole village population came into the council house. A handful of old men including the priest chief sat toward the center, and the rest of the men, old and young, seated themselves on rows of benches, each with his fellow matrilineal clansmen; the women of each clan sat apart from the men, probably to the rear. There were formal speeches by the older men, and comments by younger men. One female official, the "Pretty Woman," seems to have had an important voice in deciding the fate of prisoners brought in by a war party. Otherwise, the women exerted influence informally, through their male kinsmen. The question of war and peace was invariably among the items to be decided. In any year, the members of one clan may have been under ritual obligation to avenge a lost clansman, killed by French-allied Shawnees, while another clan may have had similar interests in going out against the English-allied Iroquois, and still another may have wished no war at all. (The handling of such relations with other Indians was greatly complicated by the necessity of maintaining trade relations with the European powers who were struggling among themselves.) Such conflicting interests within a village were quietly stated and restated, usually for days on end. Until a village sentiment crystallized and all open opposition ceased, there could be no decision.

Because political decisions had to be unanimous, the three religious ceremonies appear especially important functionally. The first ceremony helped establish a mood appropriate for the political work to follow;[3] the second interrupted the political work, probably often relieved mounting tensions, and helped assure that differences would be resolved when the council resumed.

These two rituals assisted in promoting the political mood, but other complex social machinery aided more directly. That social machinery was made up of certain kinship connections, special offices, and principles of conduct among those kin and in those offices. The social positions and the related guides for conduct caused influence to flow in systematic ways; they provided a measure of assurance that village sentiment would crystallize, and an effective village decision would be reached.

After this political work was done, the third ceremony set as its explicit task the erasing of bad feelings which might remain, and the creation of a sense of unity adequate for the implementation of the council decisions. When, for example, a general council had decided for war against some alien power, the red standard of the village was raised. The young men left their fellow clansmen, joined warriors of their respective ranks, and became the village war organization. In preparation for war, the priestly war officials conjured, warriors fasted, and a dance lasted through the night. Deeds were recounted to excite emulation. At dawn the young men went to the river and plunged seven times; again the priests conjured. The war speaker made a speech and the war party, carrying its standard and war ark, marched out of the village in a formal procession ordered by the offices and ranks of the war organization.

Here, too, was social machinery made up of social positions and related guides to conduct which helped cause authority to move in nonrandom ways. The structure provided a measure of assurance that effort would be coordinated adequately for the task at hand. That same war machinery, as directed by the councils, carried on negotiations with foreign tribes and with the colonial powers.

Means for the correct redress for murder and injury and for regulating marriage were also politically germane. Without some systematic, ongoing check on internal aggression, a village could not have joined effectively as a unit in councils, and without systematic regulation of marriage, basic political entities, the clans, could not have persisted. These tasks were handled by the several clans, almost exclusively through self-help.

These three sets of social machinery, but especially the village council and the village organization for war, were social vehicles of Cherokee village politics through the 18th century.

Early in the 18th century there was no formal political system beyond the villages. Then, the Cherokee tribe was an aggregate of politically independent villages; there were no structures to facilitate decisions by the tribe at large, or to permit the systematic coordination of tribal actions. After the creation of a tribal state at mid-century, the villages remained political entities within the larger, sovereign state.

A Cherokee state was created because, beginning in 1730, that became in-

creasingly necessary. South Carolina could cut off trade; from 1730 on, whenever Cherokee villages lost their constant supply of ammunition, they were
left exposed to armed enemy tribes. Many villages were repeatedly to suffer
from such exposure. South Carolina demanded that all Cherokees be restrained
from violence against traders and against the colonial frontier, and threatened
reprisal. From this point forward, the act of a Cherokee individual could
tangibly hurt many other Cherokees, most of whom would not know him, and
some of whom might live a hundred miles from him. As Cherokees recurrently
experienced this social fact, they responded by creating a tribal state. In effect,
South Carolina by virtue of her power was able to ascribe to the aggregate of
Cherokee villages a political unity. The tribe could become a political unit in
fact, or suffer.

The Cherokees created a state in which the major offices were held by priests.
The Cherokee priest-state was some 30 years building. In 1730, a tribal government was established which was an image of the war organizations functioning
in the villages. Its personnel were warriors, and its very limited job was negotiation with South Carolina. It could stop reprisals by punishing a guilty
Cherokee, or by handing him over to the Colony. It could not, however, prevent reprisals in the first instance, because it could not prevent misdeeds. It
could not prevent misdeeds unless it were to become tyrannical enough to
create a climate of fear. Such a tyranny did not emerge.

In the 1750's, the tribe did the next logical thing. The Cherokees created on
a tribal level the same council organization which formed and expressed public
sentiment in the villages, a tribal priest-state. For discoverable reasons, the
priest-state, like the government before it, could not adequately prevent the
young men from harming traders or raiding the frontier. After a period of success, sporadic attacks on traders and on the frontier began again, and South
Carolina, besides cutting off trade, sent white armies to burn Cherokee villages
and crops. Subsequent governmental changes brought prominent warriors into
tribal councils in the 1760's and thereby introduced new forms of coercive
discipline to Cherokee politics. The Cherokee priest-state, so modified, was able
to hold the peace until the whole country was swept into war by the American
Revolution.

The double interest of anthropology—in what is, and in what becomes or
changes—will be obvious in this study. On the one hand, there is here an attempt to describe as a single system the major parts of a political order which
existed at a point in time. That political order was the aggregate of Cherokee
villages in the early 18th century. On the other hand, this study sees that
Cherokee political order as coming to be through time something different, the
Cherokee tribal state.

In the human world, I think of three great categories of political societies:
societies where the local group is a single kin group; societies which include
numerous kin groups joined politically in single face-to-face, sovereign communities; and societies which draw into a sovereign political unit several or

many face-to-face communities and must have centralized mechanisms for exerting coercion over communities, kin groups, and individual members.[4] The second category includes the Cherokee village early in the period of this study; the third category is made up of states and includes the emerged Cherokee state as of the late 1760's.

My intent is to describe. A historian will not think this a good description; it holds to a very abstract, analytic plane, with concrete actions by particular men entering only to serve as evidence for classes of actions by classes of men. The reason is only partly that I deal here with historical records which are thin, and that anthropologists usually do not have the practiced patience of historians to wring the most from even thin records. The more essential reason is that I write primarily to offer a model for other possible descriptions, including, perhaps, someone's future and better description of 18th century Cherokee political life.

I offer this form of thought, this manner of reading group life, because I hope it can draw together kinds of phenomena which anthropology does not usually join, or join well. I attempt here to connect social structure, ethos, and personality. The reader will find in this form of thought, I believe, a place for every fact of interest to students of social structure, including several kinds of relevant fact glossed over or unreported altogether in social structure studies. I believe he will find also a place for every fact of interest to students of ethos— of patterns of valuing behavior in the relations among men. He will find those two bodies of fact, structure and ethos, here interconnected, as they are joined in human behavior before separation by the intellects of observers.

Social structure and ethos are here put down in a manner which connects them one to the other. Beyond that, those facts are put down, by the form of thought here suggested, in a way which builds a bridge to studies of the human individual

The distinction between "individual" and "person" (however that distinction might variously be phrased) appears to be the essential foundation upon which all sciences of human behavior build. The notion of individual focuses on experiencing organisms; human organisms are born with genetic equipment, live some while subject to biological laws and to experience, and assume thereby shape and character, and die. Studies in terms of the idea of individual necessarily attend the human life career, whole careers, or parts of careers of some duration. The notion of person focuses on enduring ideas shared by members of a society; a person is an idea, a social invention handed down by tradition, and in that sense deathless. These shared ideas identify a man to his fellows as first one social thing then another—as brother, old man, wolf clansman— according to the situation. Ideas about persons order a society as personnel. Any particular man is thought of as many persons by his fellows and by himself; any particular person is thought to identify many different men, usually many at one moment (but if not, then one at one time, and another later). When one describes social structure or ethos, one describes it in terms of the

notion of person. Ethos and social structure, each in its different manner, describe a people's normative ideas about themselves. Both describe a people's
traditional thoughts about themselves as personnel. The form of thought here
offered puts down such normative person-facts in a manner which permits that
they readily be translated into individual-facts of experience and expression,
to be joined with other such individual-facts and possibly to permit new under-
standings of the human personality.

This wedding of person-facts to individual-facts appears possible because
social structure and ethos are here put down in a manner which holds in close
focus the long-recognized fact that the various personnel arrangements of any
society occur in a nonrandom recurrent sequence; each arrangement has its
several turns through (often) an annual cycle. In any society a particular personnel arrangment follows some other, lasts some moments, days or weeks, is
succeeded by still another, and reoccurs on later predictable occasions as some
regular round of social life unfolds. As here put down, person-facts are described so as to hold in focus the duration of any given arrangement and the
juxtaposition of that arrangement with others. So described, person-facts are
laid out as they are recurrently experienced by men, and as they recurrently
offer opportunity for the expression of the psychic needs of men, or hinder such
expression.

Insofar as the mode of description here demonstrated might prove to grasp
these larger bodies of fact and put them in important interconnection, it does so
with economic simplicity and with a rightful regard for the traditions of holistic
anthropological inquiry. This study stands in the British tradition in its handling of social structure, and in the American tradition in its handling of ethos
and its concern for personality. These three conceptual tools, social structure,
ethos, and personality, represent the best of anthropological efforts to characterize human societies holistically—as systems of interconnected parts. This is,
therefore, a conservative study which draws together earlier and larger efforts
and, by putting them together, perhaps makes something slightly new of each.
Redfield said, "We do not enact a science: It grows." Perhaps these pages contain an early partial awareness of some aspects of growth which has been occurring, unbidden and but vaguely felt. One may hope to have accurately recognized such growth.

I offer a name for this manner of describing group life; my analysis is guided
by the notion of "structural pose."

The major intent is to suggest a manner of describing, hence that which is
here described—Cherokee political life—takes secondary importance. For that
reason, I do not restrict myself to telling only about those ethnographic facts
which admit of virtual documentary proof. I fill in, infer, speculate to a degree
which cannot but do frequent violence to the particular realities which were
Cherokee life. I do so because my major intent can be served only if a system is
described in much of its totality. Put otherwise, I imagine my responsibilities
to historical scholarship to be limited and those limited responsibilities to be

acquitted by candor: throughout I attempt to keep explicit the relationship of ethnographic facts to interpretation. Some assertions are based on facts backed by documentary evidence; they are simply stated with the relevant citations. Other assertions are permissible inferences from such reliable facts; others are more remote inferences, easily questionable; some central assertions are mere assumptions with little documentary support and occasionally none at all. I try always to say which is which.

Structural pose is a manner of reading a group's life. This study recommends the notion of structural pose for the characterization of not too complex living societies.

PART I
THE FACE-TO-FACE COMMUNITY

It is by . . . native politeness
alone . . . that the chiefs bind the
hearts of their subjects, and carry
them wherever they will.
(Payne MS, IVb:66)

Each triangle represents an ideal population pyramid of male villagers (horizontal dimension represents numbers of men, vertical dimension represents age). Person and role sets internal to the groups depicted here are described in the text.

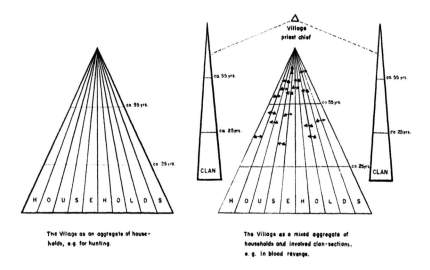

The Village as an aggregate of house-holds, e.g. for hunting.

The Village as a mixed aggregate of households and involved clan-sections, e. g. in blood revenge.

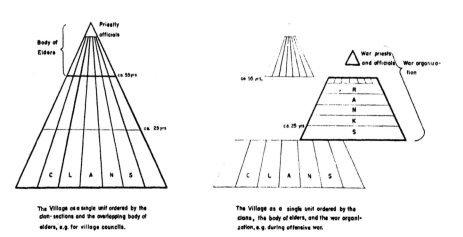

The Village as a single unit ordered by the clan-sections and the overlapping body of elders, e.g. for village councils.

The Village as a single unit ordered by the clans, the body of elders, and the war organi-zation, e.g. during offensive war.

FIG. 2. Four structural poses: the sets of persons and roles available to a Cherokee village for male work.

CHAPTER 1

One Village: Four Village Structures

THROUGH the year, largely according to the seasons, a round of male tasks unfolded in each Cherokee village. Each recurrent task was, to each man of a village, a signal. When the white flag, for example, was raised over a village council house to call a village council, a young male villager was aware, with little thought, that he was now expected to assume a defined set of relationships with every other villager. At the moment before, perhaps his significant relations had been with other young men of his household, the extended household of his wife's family; then, the men of his clan had been similarly dispersed to the households of their wives severally occupied with diverse household interests; the total village was, as personnel, sorted according to household. Now, when the white flag was raised, his clansmen were expected to come bodily together, his more significant relations were expected to be with these clansmen who were now occupied with him in a single common task as a corporate group among other like groups; the total village, as personnel, was sorted according to clan. In one village activity, one combination of relations was considered to be operative; in another activity, a different combination. The total village population sorted and resorted itself in four different structures, according to the activity at hand. A schematic diagram of these four "structural poses" is given in Figure 2. This chapter introduces these four structures.[5]

This chapter describes ideas shared by the men of a Cherokee village about how they ought to sort themselves as personnel; it deals with "persons." A person is a shared idea, a device used by a people to sort themselves; it is an imagined social niche (warrior, clan brother, father) publicly recognized by tradition to exist, and, on set recurrent occasions, recommended to sundry men as the appropriate social thing for them to be. Every people recurrently sort and resort themselves in some such manner. Person, the recommended social niche, is but one side of a coin. The opposite side is role, the rules for public conduct held up by society as appropriate for the men who are in each social niche. In the course of a day, it is suggested to any man in any society that he be many persons-with-roles, usually one at a time or in combinations which do not conflict. A society's total system of persons and roles is, as the term is used here, its social structure. This chapter deals with persons only—with recommended social niches as such—and makes very little reference to roles, the corresponding norms of conduct recommended by villagers to each other.[6]

Person and role are separated here only to permit some economy in describing the Cherokee structure for politics. In the observed world there are behaving men who have thoughts in their heads, including thoughts about what person each man should in a given context be, and about the role such a kind of man might be expected properly to play. Such thoughts are conscious to the actors or easily made conscious, for example, when another's public actions depart from what is by tradition expected. However, such shared ideas about person (who a man appropriately is) and about role (how that kind of man should behave) are, to the actors, not often separated, and are separated here only temporarily, to be rejoined in subsequent chapters.

An observer knows he has identified an imagined social niche when we recognize two contrasting patterns of recommended conduct. That is, in the sense followed here, there cannot be two persons with a single role, nor a single person with two roles, for these identify one another. A single role may be compounded so as to include alternative courses of appropriate action, and all roles seem to include a permissible range of conduct. In this complex sense, persons and roles are but opposite aspects of a single social thing. The vocabulary of a people (warrior, clan brother, etc.) closely approximates but never exactly duplicates the battery of persons used by the people to sort themselves in ordering their group life; the only index which identifies a person is a corresponding role.

One identifies persons and roles in living societies by keeping an eye simultaneously on action and reaction. One seeks to find similar patterns of action among men in a society which evoke consistently more or less approving reactions; these observations reveal, grossly at first, certain ideas of the actors— selected persons and roles imagined by that people. The identification is further checked by seeing that in the same kind of context consistent departures from those patterns of action consistently evoke some measure of disapproval. Usually one gets further confirmation and leads as to further details by asking the people to explain why a man behaved as he did.

Of all behavior, some has such public meaning. In this study, the interest is in this kind of public behavior, in actions done (conformingly or otherwise) with an eye to a valuing audience, the fellow members of a society. Persons and roles are the enduring value thoughts behind such public behavior. The social structure here described is an ordering of those value thoughts.[7]

This study does not deal with a living society, hence I cannot observe action and reaction and thereby infer the value thoughts of Cherokee actors. The procedure here is a substitute which contains some peril. The record provides assertions about consistent patterns of Cherokee behavior: the priests are circumspect toward others; clan brothers morally censure one another through boisterous joking. Such reported behavior (taken alone as it must often be) could reflect mere habit, or other behavior unmindful of a valuing audience. However, at some risk such observations are reinterpreted to say the following: *if* two men from a single clan met, and *if* one was deemed at that moment to be priest (and not clan brother), and *if* that one acted circumspectly, then Cherokees would have approved. Thereby, I imagine that I have identified a person (priest) and the gross outlines of the corresponding role (circumspect behavior); analogously, I imagine that I could also identify the contrasting person, clan brother, and its role.

This chapter introduces the notion of structual pose (Gearing 1958) which makes possible all that will follow in the study. A structural pose is the way a simple human society sees itself to be appropriately organized at a particular moment for a particular purpose. The notion of structural pose presents a frame for the orderly description of a people's valuings about human relations: it gathers and orders persons and roles. Structural pose does not attempt to describe actual behavior. It cannot, by itself, explain behavior. The social structure of male Cherokee villagers was four structural poses (possibly five) which appeared recurrently through a Cherokee year, each in its several turns according to the village tasks at hand.

The notion of structural pose makes us ask: for any given Cherokee task (pushing aside everything we might know about other Cherokee tasks), *what was the universe of available persons?* With that set of traditionally imagined niches, and only that set, the total village considered itself appropriately arranged as personnel for the task at hand. I shall in the next pages put it slightly differently, to simplify the telling. I shall usually look through the eyes of some one young Cherokee man as he faced with his fellows each task in the round of male work, and, through his eyes, I shall identify the whole village male population as persons appropriately related to him and he to them at that moment.

Among Cherokee villagers, who were a face-to-face community, every man was several persons to every other man. The notion of structural pose requires that one ask as between any two men at any one moment: of the many persons they could be, one to the other, which did their fellows recommend that they publicly be?

The chapter describes, then, certain ideas, in 18th century Cherokee minds, which male villagers brought to their various recurrent tasks. These ideas allowed some 130 adult males, faced with one village task, to sort themselves as one set of persons, and allowed those same men, for another task, to re-sort themselves. There were four such sets of persons; each set was considered appropriate in turn as the annual round of male tasks unfolded.

Kinship, sex, and age were the constants of village structure. When father and son, for example, were put together, that kinship relation always recommended to them certain behavior and disallowed other behavior. However, one structural pose brought them together while others held them apart: they were usually together when the household operated, and necessarily apart, for example, when the clans were gathered. Such coming together and parting could be but was not always a matter of physical space. There follows brief mention of these three sets of structural constants. They were the raw materials to be used by Cherokees in the four structural poses as needed.

The aboriginal Cherokee kinship system was a Crow-type system. The more significant kinship terms are shown in English translation on the diagrams of Figures 3, 4, and 5.[8]

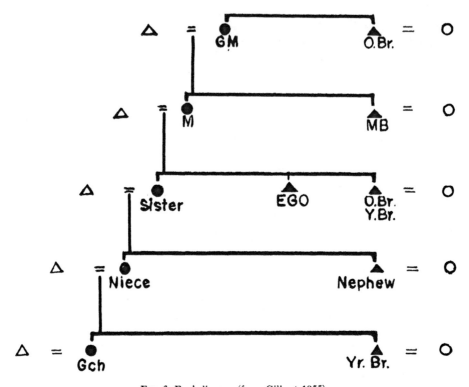

FIG. 3. Ego's lineage (from Gilbert 1955).

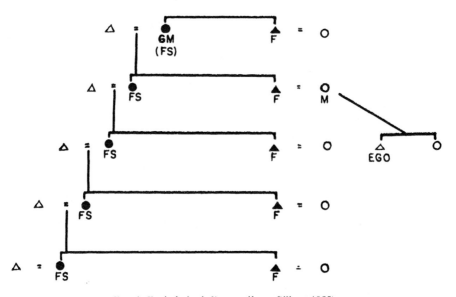

FIG. 4. Ego's father's lineage (from Gilbert 1955).

MOTHER'S FATHER'S LINEAGE

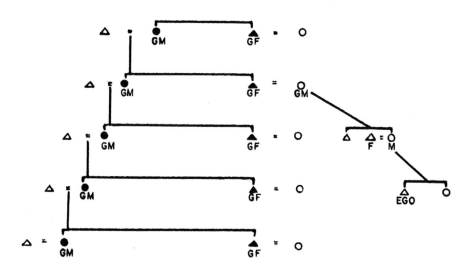

FATHER'S FATHER'S LINEAGE

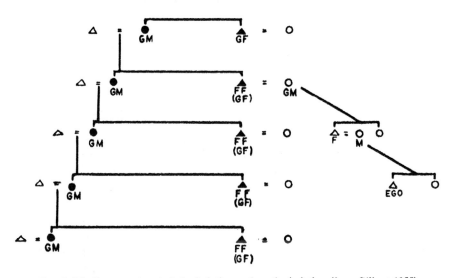

FIG. 5. The lineages of ego's father's father and mother's father (from Gilbert 1955).

Cherokee distinctions in terms of sex and age were expected also to affect behavior whenever any two Cherokees were brought together. Two sex statuses were employed. The sexual division of labor was rather thorough, but certain phases of agricultural labor fell to the men, and female warriors apparently existed under rare circumstances. Male age statuses after infancy were boy, young man, and beloved man. Specific acts, probably initiated by the individuals themselves, signaled the fact of transition. Between 20 and 30 years of age most boys established a family and thus passed into the status of young man. Between 50 and 60 years of age most young men ceased to join war parties and thus became beloved men. The age status beloved man carried much prestige and influence.

I describe now four sets of persons available to male Cherokee villagers to accomplish their various tasks.

A young Cherokee spent most of the hours of the year with members of his household. With these he usually ate and slept and attended to most of his bodily needs. With the males of the household he performed the largest economic task, the hunt. For the hunt and for other household tasks, the Cherokee village was an aggregate of independent households. (I do not treat here special hunts to gather meat for the major village ceremonies; these were organized differently, as an aspect of village organization for major ceremonies.) By Cherokee reckoning there were two seasons, winter and summer. Beginning soon after the Cherokee New Year in October, young men in small parties, usually less than 10 individuals intermittently left the village for a series of winter hunts. The principal prey was deer; deer meat was a major food, and deer hides the major trade item. Hunters usually stalked their prey; hence there was no premium on large parties, and success depended less on coordination of the group than on individual skill. If the hunt should take men into the area of hostile tribes, parties would tend to be larger for safety. Religious ceremonies in April marked the end of winter and of the winter hunting season. Between planting and harvest, the young men again went out, this time for shorter summer hunts.

The small hunting parties typically included the young men of one or possibly a very few households, probably joined on some occasions by any beloved men of the household still able to stand the rigors of the trip. The division of labor—who should hunt and who not—was an internal household matter. The relations among members of hunting parties were almost exclusively a household matter (and at most a matter of loose coordination among parties from a few households). The disposal of the catch was a household matter.

A young husband and father, as he recurrently faced hunting and other household tasks, found it necessary to get along with the members of the usual extended, matrilocal, Cherokee family. He was in direct relationship with his wife, their children, and usually with certain members of his wife's family: her parents, her sisters, their husbands and children, and her unmarried brothers. Cherokee tradition recommended to a young husband doing household tasks that this household be his significant universe, and among the members of the household there necessarily developed a sense of shared responsibility and pooled interest in respect to household work. Other villagers outside the household, including the blood kin of a young husband, became a collective audience before which he and his household jointly performed. That audience was itself similarly divided into households and similarly preoccupied. Relations with men in that larger audience certainly occurred in the course of performing household tasks; but those outside relations were deemed extraneous and compared to the interaction among members of the household were both infrequent and haphazard. The work depended upon the household relations; they were patterned in a manner which appears to have effectively accomplished that work.

For a young husband, the in-laws, male and female, were sorted as but five kinds of kin whom he addressed in terms which roughly translate:

> wife
> child (sons and daughters)[9]
> parent-in-law (wife's mother and father)
> relative-in-law (wife's brothers and sisters)
> like brother (wife's sisters' husbands)

Toward each of those five kin contrasting patterns of behavior were expected, hence these kin terms mark off five persons. However, three of these must be further distinguished as to sex; hence, each of these three kin terms stands for two different structural niches. A young husband was expected to act differently toward his son as against his daughter (both termed "child"), toward his wife's father as against her mother (both "parent-in-law"), and toward his wife's brothers as against her sisters (both "relative-in-law"). These distinctions would be required in virtue of the pervasive sexual division of labor, for example. In the sense used in this study, person and role define one another, and it is not expected that a people's vocabulary perfectly reflects their battery of persons-with-roles. Hence, as seen by a young husband, the members of his household were sorted as eight kinds of person. His society expected that in his public behavior he take cognizance of the kind of person each member of the household was.

A young husband was instructed by his society that certain tasks were the exclusive affair of his household. Members of other households were expected not to interfere; conversely, he was not to interfere with other households as they independently went about those same tasks. These other villagers were, however, an audience. If a young man consistently behaved well toward those eight kinds of persons making up his household, this audience expressed diffuse approval by holding him on that count in esteem; if he behaved poorly, this audience was ready to hear and repeat gossip, and his repute suffered. This audience was not a faceless mass; for example, the disapproval of a sister was extremely painful. But such differentiation was on the level of private sentiment and nonpublic behavior. In terms of normative structure, a man's sister was not differentiated in this context from other villagers. Such a sister was expected publicly not to interfere, nor was any other villager, in this household domain.[10]

In these terms, a young husband engaged in household work was expected to see villagers outside the household as a single kind of person; I shall call this person:

other householder.

Seen through the eyes of a young husband, then, the universe of operative persons in his household, male and female, was nine. The universe of persons for other members of his household, for example his wife, was analogous.

Only the men of a household did the hunting. To a young husband, these males were the four male persons named above. The coordination of their efforts was assisted by recommended patterns of kinship behavior, held up by the society at large as appropriate. For example, a man was expected to teach his male child hunting skills; in general he was expected to be a kindly, respected helper and teacher, and was not expected to discipline the child (since that fell to the mother's brother). A man was expected to demonstrate respect for his male parent-in-law. A man was expected to joke with his wife's brothers and her sisters' husbands. These last were approximate age mates of young to middle years, and to them and him fell the brunt of the physical labor connected with hunting. A joke is an excellent device for bringing erring or recalcitrant individuals into line; it was so used in other areas of Cherokee life and probably among these persons also.

I have named nine structural niches as seen by a young man. These formed the universe of persons considered by his society as appropriate for him during the handling of household work. I have not dealt with the similar sets of niches as viewed by his wife or male parent-in-law or other members of the household, and have but cursorily alluded to the roles which correspond to each person. Nor will these matters receive further treatment in these pages. Household tasks were left to the aggregate of village households working independently of each other, all serving each merely as structurally undifferentiated audience. By definition, such activities are not political. This structural pose serves, then, as backdrop to village politics.

On occasion, some of the Cherokee households were expected temporarily to separate. For example, in the event of a killing or injury of or by a fellow clansman, a man was expected to leave household work and to join his clansmen.[11] For purposes of punishing a killer, and for other purposes, the village assumed this second structural pose. For this task and others, certain clan sections became the significant groups, and the village became an aggregate including at least two activated clan sections, with the topmost village priestly official assigned to intercede between opposed clans; villagers not members of the involved clans remained sorted as to their respective households.

Membership in the clan was ascribed matrilineally as suggested by the Crow kinship terminology. There were seven Cherokee clans, and it is reported (leaving some mystery) that every village had all seven represented. The clansmen within a village formed, when they acted together, a corporate group.[12] I call that local clan group a clan section.

To the clan sections, acting as independent corporate units, fell three major tasks. First, clan sections were the landholding units; garden plots were allocated by each clan section to the households of the clan women.

Second, to the clan sections fell the responsibility of regulating marriage. A person could not marry into his own clan or into his father's clan;[13] it was preferred that a man marry into his father's father's or mother's father's clans. Widows were often expected to marry their dead husband's brother, and widowers their dead wife's sister. The regulation of marriage included the proper selection of a mate; the men of a clan section punished fellow clansmen for infractions or for threatened infractions. Legitimate marriages were ceremonially recognized by the topmost village official. Marriage was further regulated by women "in the town" [read: fellow clanswomen] (Payne MS, IVb:277) through punishment of widows or widowers for violations of mourning regulations, and through the mutual support among clanswomen against men who deserted or grossly neglected their wives and children; in both instances women publicly fell upon the wrong-doers and whipped them.

Due to Cherokee marriage patterns, membership in a local clan section was for married men often not a matter of literal kinship. In villages of about 400 there might be at any moment some 30 marriageable girls; Cherokee incest laws prohibited marriage with about two-sevenths of these 30, leaving by generous reckoning only some 20–25 eligible mates. There were no recorded rules or preferences as to village endogamy, and several particular instances are recorded of men who married into other villages. It seems to follow that men often married women from appropriate clans but outside their villages. When men did so, they usually took up residence in the village and household of their wives. In such instances a man became a member of the section of his clan in his new village. The fellow clansmen in his new village automatically were clan brothers to him, but it could often be that none or very few of these new relatives were traceably related to him genealogically.

The third task that fell to the clan sections was the orderly resolution of aggression between villagers. Murder required blood revenge.[14] The clan section was for this task a corporate individual; all clansmen were guilty if a clansman had killed, and all male clansmen were responsible for revenge if a clansman had been killed. The killer or one of his clan was killed if it was thought he had murdered intentionally; otherwise, less drastic modes of settlement were possible. A guilty party fled, if he could, to the house of the village priest chief where he could not be killed. Here the two clan sections held a hearing and, for crimes short of murder, arranged a settlement. Probably, theft and bodily injury were handled in similar manner.

Of these three tasks, none are properly political in the sense followed in this study: in none of these did the village act as a single unit; rather, duties were delegated to lesser units, the clan sections, which acted independently. However, two of these tasks were politically germane in that were they not performed the village population would have been greatly hindered in its political work, such as in council. Were marriage not regulated, primarily in respect to the enforcement of rules of clan exogamy, the clan sections could not have endured and clan sections were, as will be seen, essential units during village councils. Similarly, were extreme aggression between villagers not checked and resolved through orderly procedure, the village population would have found it impossible or unusually difficult to join in the give-and-take inherently necessary in reaching final village-wide judgments in council or to coordinate wars and negotiations.

The regulation of marriage and control of aggression were prerequisites for Cherokee political work. The importance of these tasks and the public concern that they be accomplished is perhaps evidenced by the fact that in both instances the foremost village official, the village priest chief was often involved, acting as if clanless and on behalf of the total village.

During these three tasks, clan sections were independent corporate groups. The universe of persons among male clansmen was remarkably small. Within his traceable matrilineal lineage, a man could have but four kinds of male relatives:

> mother's brother (his mothers' brothers)
> nephew (his sisters' sons)
> older brother (brothers and mothers' mothers' brothers)
> younger brother (brothers and sisters' daughters' sons).[15]

Beyond the lineage, all male clansmen were fictive brothers; recommended conduct toward these fictive brothers appears different from recommended conduct toward real brothers, hence it is necessary to add fictive brothers as a separate person:

> clan brother.

This set of persons could act as a tightly disciplined unit in virtue of the patterns of conduct recommended by Cherokee society among these kin. The mother's brother could require that he be highly respected by his adult nephew. A brother was expected to censure his brother for wrong conduct by making public jokes at his expense. (I shall return to the efficient coordination possible inside a clan section when I treat the village councils in Chapter 3. It will be apparent there that I have oversimplified in this context, for brevity, by not dealing with the significant fact that, in any pair of kin, one or both or neither might be of the age-status beloved man as against young man.)

Since in blood revenge and the regulation of marriage, a clan section necessarily acted in opposition to some other corporate clan section, it is not possible simply to consider the remaining villagers as a single kind of person. Rather, they were two:

opposed clansman
uninvolved villager.

Finally, for his potential mediation sometimes utilized, one final person must be added:

priest chief.

In sum, the universe of male persons for the duration of these tasks totaled eight; at these moments, in the eyes of an acting Cherokee man, his village was so sorted. The universe of persons for the women was analogous.

Yet this is too simple. In any instance of clan revenge, it is virtually certain that at least one member of a revenging clan section would be married into a household of the clan section of the murderer. It is difficult to imagine that he could be unmindful of his own sons who in principle shared the corporate guilt and were subject to be killed, and that that compelling sentiment was not publicly recognized and publicly handled through structural arrangement. It is, however, unrecorded what public cognizance Cherokees took of that human fact.

The structural pose for handling internal aggression and regulating marriage could well be described in further detail in a study of politics, since these tasks, while not narrowly political, were politically germane. This study, however, passes it quickly by.

A third set of social niches, a third structural pose, was considered appropriate for village council. For purposes of making certain necessary decisions, each Cherokee village became a single organized whole, hence acted politically. These decisions included primarily matters of relations with alien tribes, and trade and alliances with European colonies. They probably also included internal affairs, such as a decision to move the village when land became exhausted, or to build or repair public buildings.

Villagers organized themselves into a single whole by becoming a set of seven clan sections and by activating also another organized group which cut across the seven clans, the body of elders. (This term is mine; Cherokees referred to this body as "the beloved men.") The body of elders contained all villagers of the age status beloved man. The foremost officials were the priest chief with three other priests and one secular officer. These five men lived near the council house and probably acted during general councils as if they were without clan affiliation. Other beloved men formed a second order of officials who were regarded simultaneously as clansmen in their respective clans and members of the crosscutting body of elders. These were the priest chief's seven-man inner council of clansmen. One man was drawn from each clan section, and each was the voice of his clan section during the councils. The remaining beloved men were a third order of officials in the body of elders. These men, like the inner council, acted during councils both as clansmen and as elders. The re-

maining men of the village, men in the age status of young man, were differentiated by clan.[16]

The physical seating arrangements in council reflected these structural
facts. All the village—men, women and probably children, some 400 in all—
came into the council house when the white standard which announced councils
(and ceremonials) was raised. The priest chief and his priestly and secular
officials sat on special benches toward the center as did the seven-man inner
council. Around the sides of the council house (some were seven-sided) sat the
rest of the population; each clan section sat together, probably with the beloved men and young men of a clan on the forward benches, and their clanswomen and children toward the rear. All male villagers could speak to points
under consideration.

The same structural arrangement served a second large purpose in village
life. In the six major religious ceremonies, the village expressed its basic ideas
about the nature of the relations between man and nature, and between man
and man. The beloved men, organized under the four main priests as the body
of elders, served the villagers who were organized as clan sections, by performing the major ritual acts of the ceremonies. For the six ceremonies held in the
village each year, the village gathered inside the council house where, as in
council, the major village officials and the inner council sat apart, and the rest
of the village was seated according to clan, men and women separated. The
body of elders also selected from the population a different set of special func-
tionaries for each festival; for the New Year ceremony, for example, the elders
appointed a group of male dancers, female dancers, a musician, a woman from
each of the seven clan sections, and a hunter from each.

The universe of male persons during councils, seen through the eyes of a
young man, was larger than the sects of persons so far considered. There were,
first, the five kinds of male relatives already encountered within a young
man's lineage and clan section:

> mother's brother
> nephew
> older brother
> younger brother
> clan brother.

Each of the seven clan sections acted corporately; a young man therefore looked
out upon his village so sorted. Hence, through his eyes, one further person must
be added.

> clansman of other clans.

These six must be further differentiated due to the fact that among them
some were older, beloved men who formed the body of elders. A young man
would not have a nephew who was a beloved man since it appears a virtual
biological impossibility that any young man could have a sister's son old enough
to be a beloved man, nor could a young man have a younger brother who was a
beloved man. But of the remaining three kinds of relatives, some usually would

be elders and others not. The historical record does not reveal in what detailed ways a young man would behave differently toward two mother's brothers, for example, one of whom was a beloved man and the other not. However, the general additional deference enjoyed by men as they moved into that status is sufficient to indicate that two mother's brothers were seen as different persons.

Among the elders there were three orders of officials. I begin with the third, most numerous, order. The five Cherokee persons listed above may be taken to refer only to relatives of the age status young man. Therefore, three additional persons (omitting nephew and younger brother) must be listed to denote similar relatives who were beloved men and of this third order of officials:

> beloved mother's brother
> beloved older brother
> beloved clan brother.

To these must be added one other person, the remaining member of this order of officials who were not of one's clan section:

> beloved man of other clans.

The second order of officials was the inner council of clansmen. As seen by a particular young man, these were two persons:

clan spokesman (This man would also be to a particular young man one of the three possible lineage kin among the beloved men, as listed above. It is completely speculative but reasonable to imagine that clan spokesmen, because of their position, put aside the various particular kin relations with fellow clansmen and treated them all as clan brothers. For this reason I enter only one person here.)

spokesman of other clans.

The first order of officials appears to have acted as if without clan affiliation and consisted, then, simply of five persons, one for each of the offices. In approximate ascending order these were:

> messenger
> keeper of the council house
> speaker
> right-hand man
> priest chief.

In sum, the universe of male persons as viewed by a young Cherokee man during councils totaled 17. The universe of male persons for old men was analogous but not identical.

Perhaps the picture is yet too simple. A man could not in council deliberations be unmindful of, for example, the sentiments of the clan section of his wife and children when those diverged from the sentiments of his own clan section. However, unlike the situation when clan revenge was at issue, these kinds of sentiments seem possibly less impelling and perhaps were not publicly admitted or, as seems more likely, were simply overridden.

With this listing of persons, I leave, for the moment, the structural pose for

village councils. This social machinery is centrally political; aided by it, Cherokee villagers formed public policy. This third structural pose will come again
under scrutiny in Chapter 3.

The Cherokee village, to carry on offensive war, assumed still a fourth
structural pose. Here the village implemented certain political decisions, hence
acted politically. When a village council had decided for war, the red standard
of the village was soon raised, and a new combination of organized groups went
into operation. Those of the age status beloved man remained organized as the
body of elders, except a very few, probably only four who removed themselves
from the elders to assume major war duties. The age status young man plus
those four beloved men plus the age status boy from adolescence on became
the village war organization. Women, children, and young men not able-
bodied acted, through clan spokesmen in both the body of elders and other
clan representatives in the war organization, as members of their several clan
sections.

The major village war officials were four beloved men with esoteric ritual
knowledge necessary for war: war chief, war priest, speaker for war, and surgeon. They were elected by the warriors. The four major war officials appointed some eight officers from the age status young man, probably *ad hoc* for
each war activity. Finally there was a seven-man council for war, one prominent warrior from each clan section. Beneath those officials, the war organization was hierarchically stratified by five war ranks which were earned through
war deeds plus an unranked class which included very young apprentice warriors and others less young but completely undistinguished in war. A Cherokee
village at full force could send in the neighborhood of 100 warriors into the field.
(Mention should also be made of "war women." On the return of war parties,
these women became a part of the war organization and had a large voice in
determining whether hostages would be killed or adopted. It is probable that
they acted as clanswomen, and that their decisions were based on the ritual
necessities of revenge for lost clansmen.)

It would be without point to list the universe of male persons available for
ordering war activities. The list would be enormous, and the essential point
which must here be made concerns the very size of this set of persons. There
were the 11 persons already described within the body of elders. Within the
war organization itself two further series of persons are apparent. Twenty-five
are implied by the above comments on war offices and ranks. Then, the full
web of male kinship was deemed operative, and it is clear that any man
might expect to have at least 10 kinds of kin present, counting only those male
kin in his own and one adjoining generation. For any one man, the total set of
possible persons inside the war organization would be close to 250, virtually the
product of the first and second series of persons.[17] That potential total within
the war organization was twice the size of any possible village war party.

Clearly, this fourth structural pose was a social order different in kind from
the first three. It was a social order which relative to the others lacks structural

precision. Lacking precision, it probably lacked utility. Later, in Chapter 4, I shall ask why this imprecision existed. I shall seek also to learn how, if not by social structure, the behavior of war parties was patterned and controlled; my answer will be that war parties were pecking orders, ordered by personality, in which big and aggressive men lorded it over small and less aggressive men, illegitimately and without much correspondence with the system of persons-with-role which nominally applied.

In actual fact, this nominal organization was but little used as a total unit. The size of war parties was usually between 20 and 40 men (Adair 1775:382). If all the village warriors did go against a single enemy, they usually divided into a number of companies which operated independently.

Three other village activities had available similar village structures. Rather than decide for war with a particular tribe or colony, the village general council might decide to send a party to negotiate. Such parties, numbering usually 15 or 20, were drawn from the age status young man, and the relationships among members of the party were the same that held among those persons during offensive war. Most negotiating parties went out soon after the New Year village council. These parties carried with them instructions from the council and, unlike war parties, were usually able to maintain close communication with the body of elders during negotiations. Hence, the formal authority of the body of elders over these negotiating parties was more than nominal, unlike its authority over most war parties.

Periodically, during the summer when warfare was rare, the young men joined together for ballplays with other villages. They assumed then a set of relations with one another, and with the village at large, which was analogous to the structure of the village for war.

In the event of attack on a village by an enemy, the village was willy-nilly organized under the war organization hierarchy. In these crises, warriors rallied around war leaders; the women, children, and old men fled together into hiding when that was possible, while war leaders tried to maintain order and discipline adequate for defense and counter attack.

The set of social niches nominally available to order war activities was inherently unworkable. Such a magnitude of possible niches seems to create no social map to the actors which permits each man clearly to know who, in structural terms, every other man is, to have expectations in virtue of that knowledge, and to enjoy the support of fellows should his expectations not be met. In the context of such structural confusion, other determinants of human behavior might have freer rein, in this case personality variables as will later be seen. All behavior of human groups is patterned, none is fully random. But that patterning need not stem in all instances from social structure.

The inherent illogic of this set of structural positions does not become apparent in the listing of war offices and ranks. Nor would it become unmistakable by the additional mention of relevant kinship positions. That illogic does become unavoidably apparent when one asks the tedious question asked throughout this chapter: What is the universe of persons recommended to the actors for the work at hand? The question requires that the total population be identified—every actor as some one social thing to every other, at the moment, and for the purposes at hand. In simple societies, when this cannot be done the data are not yet in. If it is done and the resulting image is unworkable, the data are wrong or, as I believe in the present case, the behavior in question is not much ordered by social structure.

This structural pose for war appears to have been as real as any of the previous poses. That is, it appears to have existed, as all structural facts (as that term is used in these pages), as ideas about persons and roles in the minds of Cherokees. Cherokees described these structural facts to Buttrick in much detail, and to others. The point is, these ideas did little work—they affected behavior but little. Social structure never affects behavior categorically since personality and interests always have their competing effects. But in the instance before us, social structure seems to have affected behavior almost not at all, and haphazardly. The source of the regularity in Cherokee war behavior must be sought elsewhere.

I mention very briefly the possibility of a fifth Cherokee structural pose. The records are ambiguous; hence this fifth set of persons cannot be reported as fact. In this pose certain phases of agricultural work and other tasks may have been done. Here, the four foremost priests performed priestly services for the several households and, through an additional appointed foreman, sometimes directed all the households in collective work (Adair 1775:430; Payne MS, IVa:27).

These priests ritually determined when the planting should begin. Through an appointed foreman they directed the various households who collectively planted all the household plots. During the growing season there were further services in ritual control of the weather, and at least some of the cultivation of the plots was done collectively. There is little question that such ritual assistance and cooperative labor occurred; possibly these were organized by the structure here suggested. Harvests, however, were handled independently by the several households, and some of the crop was put in public granaries for the use and disposition of the priests.

Probably two other services were performed for the several households by these four priests. First, there are ambiguous reports of priestly services to hunters; certainly there was esoteric magic performed to insure the kill. Possibly, these services were performed in this fifth possible pose. Second, when a death occurred, a priest, "appointed by the town," was called. All household furnishings were buried or destroyed, and the priest cleansed the house. After four days the

right hand man then sent a messenger to this family, with a piece of tobacco to enlighten their eyes, and a strand of beads to comfort their hearts and a request for them to take their seats in the council house that night . . . where all the town met them, and took them by the hand (Payne MS, III:35; and IVb:272–73).

Probably one other body of work was directed by the priests through the appointed foreman. I allude to the construction and repair of public buildings.

Figure 2 depicts four sets of persons available to the men of a Cherokee village in their annual round of recurrent activities. In all village activities, age, sex, and kinship strongly influenced villagers' expectations of one another. In addition, villagers joined together in organized groups, which were formed or not formed with reference to the tasks at hand. In terms of these organized groups and the persons they brought together, the annual cycle of Cherokee village events called into being four structural poses.

A structural pose is, then, the way a simple human society sees itself to be appropriately organized at a moment. The social structure of such a human group is the rhythmic way each structural pose materializes in its turn, according to the tasks at hand. For Cherokee men, there were four (possibly five) such poses; for Cherokee men, the rhythmic sequence of male tasks, hence the rhythmic sequence from each pose to the next, was established in large part by the annual round of seasons. The rhythm of social structure for Cherokee male work is schematically depicted by Figure 6.

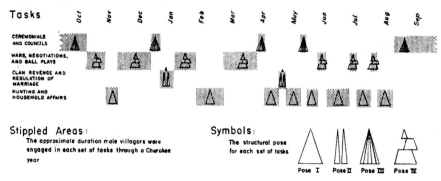

Fig. 6. The rhythm of Cherokee social structure for male work (schematic).

Cherokee women have been left to one side. Their tasks moved in different rhythms; as I dimly see it, those tasks were performed largely, but not exclusively, in a pose which sorted them as independent households. A full description of the social structure for Cherokee village life would discover both sets of poses, each moving in its own rhythm, and depict the combinations which occurred in a Cherokee year, or lifetime.

When any community, acting as a single organized group, makes decisions, it is acting politically. The implementation of those political decisions, whether or not that is done by the village acting as a single unit, is political action. Of the four sets of tasks of Cherokee village men, two were political. Hunting was not political action since the total village did not act as a unit but as an aggregate of households. The control of aggression and the regulation of marriage were prerequisites for village politics but, since the village did not act as a unit, were not narrowly political activities. Councils and offensive war and negotiation were political activities. Under the structural pose assumed during general councils, male villagers made their major decisions, and under the structural pose assumed for offensive war and negotiation, they implemented some of the more difficult of those decisions.

CHAPTER 2

The Cherokee Ethos

IN ANY description of Cherokee social structure, one would mention certain rules about appropriateness and decency in human relations—in other words, Cherokee notions about good men. One would include thus roles recommended of persons. These same rules are the phenomena examined if one inquires as to the nature of the Cherokee ethos. When one inquires as to the ethos, the further question is raised whether all such Cherokee rules taken together might be found to have one focus, or a few foci, giving them a meaningful configuration; that is, all roles might be discovered to have some common quality. Employing the concept of ethos, we are led to ask about the possibility of some overriding moral sensibility among 18th century Cherokees.

Benedict's figurative phrase (1934) sends us in the right general direction; she sought some "unconscious canon of [moral] choice." Benedict, however, kept several meanings within the term ethos, two of which must be set aside at the outset. First, she moved too easily between the individual and the group. Persons and roles are group phenomena: enduring public thoughts shared by a people. Nothing reported about Cherokee person and role permits, by itself, assertions about the congeniality of those thoughts to any particular man or to any average or typical Cherokee. A man, deemed by his fellows to be a person, need only be aware that his fellows have this role expectation of him; if this is so, then this role may be put down as a real social fact. Whether that man finds that role expectation congenial, and whether all his fellows or only some of them insist, eagerly or reluctantly, upon their expectation of him, are separate and interesting questions. Ethos might be made to embrace both phenomena, the enduring public thoughts and men's receptivity to those thoughts, but the real presence of public thoughts does not permit assumptions about that congeniality. I narrow the sense of ethos. As here used, ethos includes and orders roles, enduring public thoughts about right conduct. This narrowing, I believe, facilitates the very difficult movement, in investigation, from group to individual by helping clearly to distinguish the two.

Second, Benedict spoke of a pattern of thought and action; but one cannot move easily from thought to action. Nothing reported about Cherokee person and role permits, by itself, assertions about actual Cherokee behavior. To any particular man, public thoughts about role are an aspect of his environment; at some moment of action, he knows that his fellows share certain expectations of him, relevant to the matter at hand. How he handles those expectations— his actual behavior—is, again, a separate and interesting question. Ethos could include both expectations and average or usual handling of expectations. As here used, ethos is more narrow; it includes only the role expectations.

This chapter will describe the Cherokee ethos in this narrowed meaning. I pay attention only to role, not to structural niches, and seek the overriding quality of all roles. Later, in Chapter 3, I shall again take up person, particularly that set of persons and roles available to Cherokees for councils, and I shall re-examine the Cherokee ethos in the context of the village council. From that re-examination I shall suggest a still more narrow meaning of the notion of ethos.

The single focus which created pattern in Cherokee moral thought was the value of harmony among men. The good man, in the Cherokee ideal, neither expressed anger nor gave others occasion for expressing anger.

This Cherokee ethos cannot be demonstrated directly by the historical record. Its presence can be suggested by first reviewing facts reported about contemporary Cherokee Conservatives in North Carolina,[18] and by then turning to the historical record in order to seek a measure of support for assuming that the Cherokee ethos then and now is similar in all essential respects.

About contemporary Cherokee Conservatives in North Carolina, Gulick and Thomas tell us that the "basic principle of Conservative values is Harmony." The principle explains for Cherokees much of the phenomena of nature, it defines man's place in nature, and it establishes norms of proper conduct among men. This principle of harmony appears to direct those Cherokees today, cautiously and at virtually any cost, to avoid discord. The emphasis in its application is negative—thou shalt not create disharmony—rather than positive.

The conflict disallowed in Cherokee human relations is of one kind: it is conflict between two men or several, face-to-face, open and direct. Direct, open conflict is injurious to reputation. But we read of "the great amount of malicious gossip and backbiting" and that the "services of conjurers are employed by some." We do not read that gossip is injurious to reputation, and conjuring (in most of its forms) is probably not at all hurtful to repute. Gossip and conjuring, I infer, appear to have an essential place in this harmony ethic: both seem to be means of affecting others at a distance.[19] They are weapons used by clashing wills which yet avoid face-to-face confrontation and the disallowed conflict.

This ethic, disallowing open face-to-face clashes, is operative among contemporary conservative Cherokees defining proper conduct in three contrasting situations.

First, in the usual circumstances of everyday life, one must exercise foresight so as not to intrude. The harmony ethic is maintained by the recommendation that a good Cherokee be a "quiet" man "avoiding disharmonious situations." It is maintained by not giving offense, by "the unwillingness of the individual to thrust his ideas or personality in the limelight, or to make decision for or to speak for others." We read too of a "generalized interpersonal suspiciousness" and that this may or may not be a "general cautiousness and 'feeling out' which is required by the non-interference ethic." In short, the harmony principle, in the usual run of contemporary Cherokee affairs, directs a man constantly to excercise a measure of caution because any of his particular interests may be in unrevealed conflict with the interests of his Cherokee fellows. A man is circumspect.

Second, when contrary interests do become apparent, a good man is expected "quietly [to go] his own way." One does not cease to pursue his own interests. But one takes care not directly to frustrate the actions of others and thereby avoids a confrontation, an overt clash. Primarily, one staves off threatened disharmony by "minding [his] own business."

Third, when direct conflict does inevitably occur, a good Cherokee "withdraws from it—physically if he can, emotionally if he can't." The individuals involved are considered to have acted wrongly. "Aggression of any sort (overtly hostile, competitive or self assertive) is 'giving offense.' " Withdrawal is the punishment seen as proper. A good Cherokee "does not react with counter-aggression. . . . Instead, he simply withdraws." If the offender persists, "the withdrawal develops into ostracism."

One sees, then, a characteristic web of proper relationship recommended to Cherokees: good relations are distant, cautious, quiet so as to avoid potential and apparent conflict of interest. Such moral notions, we read, are part of the cultural equipment carried by these men to their affairs. These are a standard of decency, and by this measure a man gains or fails to gain good repute. We are told this is a "first cosmic principle," pervasively applied by Cherokees, as a measure of propriety in men's behavior, but applied also, beyond that to the universe at large. The portrait, drawn by Gulick and Thomas from observations of the full complexity of ongoing Cherokee life, convinces.

The same standard of moral judgment seems to have been used by Cherokee villagers in the 18th century. The recorded evidence is much less complete than that available to Gulick and Thomas, but many points in the above portrait are supported, and there is no significant contrary evidence. In the 1700's, Cherokees appear to have recommended with equal singleness of purpose that conflict, open face-to-face clashes among fellow Cherokees, be avoided.

Indirect discord, discord at a distance, was allowed. Magic was prevalent then, more than now. Mooney (1891:322) found reasonable Haywood's earlier report that originally "Cherokees had no conception of anyone dying a natural death." Doctoring was largely a matter of counteracting spells cast by others. The intent of many spells was to compel actions in others, for example, love spells. Probably a practice described as extant just before 1900 by Mooney (1900:427) was not unlike practices of the 18th century.

The root of a plant called *unatlunwe' hitu,* "having spirals," is used in conjurations designed to predispose strangers in favor of the subject. The priest "takes it to water"— i.e., says certain prayers over it while standing close to the running stream, then chews a small piece and rubs and blows it upon the body and arms of the patient, who is supposed to start upon a journey, or to take part in a council, with the result that all who meet him or listen to his words are at once pleased with his manner and appearance, and disposed to give every assistance to his projects.

Through this or similar magic, people could be induced, apparently voluntarily, to yield to the wishes of others. Through magic, a man could gain his ends without the loss of repute which would follow repeated, open clashes.[20]

Good Cherokees in the 1700's, as today, seem to have avoided direct conflict in three ways: first, by asserting their interests cautiously; second, by turning away from impending conflict; third, by withdrawing from men who openly clashed with their fellows.

We read that in the usual run of daily affairs, quiet care was exercised to avoid intruding upon others.[21] Timberlake reports (Williams 1927:80):

> They seldom turn their eyes on the person they speak of, or address themselves to. . . . They speak so low, except in council, that they are often obliged to repeat what they were saying. . . .

There is a general theme of trickery, running through many Cherokee myths. The animals in the myths incessantly tricked one another. The rabbit and the deer matched wits (Mooney 1900:275–77): When the rabbit tried to cheat in a race and was caught, the deer won the prize (his antlers). Then the rabbit fooled the deer into letting him file his teeth sharp; instead he blunted them (hence the deer's blunt teeth). Afterwards the deer tricked the rabbit into jumping across a stream; when the rabbit jumped, the deer magically widened the stream so the rabbit could not get back. Similarly, gods were often prone to trickery and counter-trickery (Mooney 1900:256–57):

> The Sun was a young woman and lived in the East, while her brother, the Moon, lived in the West. The girl had a lover who used to come over every month in the dark of the moon to court her. He would come at night, and leave before daylight, and although she talked with him she could not see his face in the dark, and he would not tell her his name, until she was wondering all the time who it could be. At last she hit upon a plan to find out, so the next time he came, as they were sitting together in the dark of the *asi*, she slyly dipped her hand into the cinders and ashes of the fireplace and rubbed it over his face, saying, "Your face is cold; you must have suffered from the wind," and pretending to be very sorry for him, but he did not know that she had ashes on her hand. After a while he left her and went away again. The next night when the Moon came up in the sky his face was covered with spots, and then his sister knew he was the one who had been coming to see her.

People also, the myths seemed to say, were deceptive (Mooney 1900:398–99):

> There was another lazy fellow who courted a pretty girl, but she would have nothing to do with him telling him that her husband must be a good hunter or she would remain single all her life. One morning he went into the woods, and by a lucky accident managed to kill a deer. Lifting it upon his back, he carried it into the settlement, passing right by the door of the house where the girl and her mother lived. As soon as he was out of sight of the house he went by a roundabout course into the woods again and waited until evening, when he appeared with the deer on his shoulder and came down the trail past the girl's house as he had in the morning. He did this the next day, and the next, until the girl began to think he must be killing all the deer in the woods. So her mother—the old women are usually the match-makers—got ready and went to the young man's mother to talk it over. . . .

The recurrent theme of trickery in Cherokee myths suggests a pattern of Cherokee thought—a wariness about the designs of others. Possibly, these myths included symbolic restatement of the general cautiousness required among a noninterferring people.

Thus we can say that, then as now, Cherokees in everyday going and coming were expected to "exercise foresight so as not to intrude."

We find recorded evidence of a mental set to turn away from situations of impending conflict. We read (Payne MS, IVa:29) that: "In conversation, they seldom if ever contradict or censure each other. . . . "

Another theme in the myths may be a symbolic reflection of this predisposition to turn away from an unpleasant situation. For example, Mooney (1900: 258) reports a myth which explained the origin of a star constellation:

> Long ago, when the world was new, there were seven boys who used to spend all their time down by the townhouse playing the gatayu'sti game. . . . Their mothers scolded, but it did no good, so one day they collected gatayu'sti stones and boiled them in the pot with the corn for dinner. When the boys came home hungry their mothers dipped out the stones and said, "Since you like the gatayu'sti better than the cornfield, take the stones now for your dinner." The boys were very angry, and went down to the townhouse, saying "As our mothers treat us this way, let us go where we shall never trouble them any more."

Later they were lifted into the sky and became the constellation. Again, similarly (Mooney 1900:304):

> There was a boy who used to go bird hunting every day, and all the birds he brought home he gave to his grandmother, who was very fond of him. This made the rest of the family jealous, and they treated him in such a fashion that at last one day he told his grandmother he would leave them all, but that she must not grieve for him.

Finally, the myth referred to earlier explained the movement of the sun and moon relative to one another. The moon was brother to the sun and had seduced her before she discovered his identity (Mooney 1900:257):

> He was so much ashamed to have her know it that he kept as far away as he could at the other end of the sky all night. Ever since he tries to keep a long way behind the Sun, and when he does sometimes have to come near her in the west, he makes himself as thin as a ribbon so that he can hardly be seen.

The desirability of avoiding conflict is indicated in the third major ceremony which was devoted to wiping out bad feeling. Bad feeling was a social wrong and was associated with physical disease and pollution.[22]

A Buttrick informant (Payne MS, IVb:209–10) asserted that the word *nuwoti* meant a power that heals disease, and a power that expiates [social] guilt or moral pollution. The same association is seen in a second purpose the above ceremony could serve: at the time of its regular occurrence in the village annual cycle, it celebrated the unity among villagers, but it was also called to combat epidemics. A Buttrick informant reported (Payne MS, III:32):

> When any town was visited with some fatal disease the people supposed some evil

nanehi had destroyed the efficacy of the medicine. And other towns, fearing a like calamity celebrated the [ceremony] in order to please God and lead Him to defend them them from so great a clamity.

Bad thoughts toward others were treated with the same medicines used for certain physical ills. In 1758 an English trader killed a Cherokee. Relations with South Carolina were then quite uneasy, and both sides feared the event might touch off war. A Cherokee warrior reported to Captain Demere, stationed in Cherokee country, that a priest chief had sent to a cousin of the dead man a "physic" to wash with so "he might be cleansed from all bad thoughts. . . . He accepted the physic and now his thoughts and words are the same" (Jenkins 1949: March 3, 1758).[23]

Perhaps we can say that, then as now, a good Cherokee "quietly [went] his own way."

In the face of most kinds of open, disruptive clashes, good Cherokees in the 1700's probably punished by withdrawing, but in this respect the record is very weak. Later I shall relate an instance where the behavior of a Cherokee was disruptive and his fellow villagers withdrew from him, finally ostracizing him. (See the story of Mankiller of Tellico, Chapters 5 and 7.) But the discovery of such dynamics would require the recording of a series of connected events, stretching over weeks or months; such recording rarely occurred. It must also be remembered that withdrawal and even ostracism could be very difficult for an outsider to notice—a matter of unresponsive facial expression, perhaps.

Possibly this predisposition to withdraw also received symbolic expression. Cherokee villagers seem to have characteristically visualized their relations with other villagers in terms of physical distance. That visual image is suggested by phrases habitually used by Cherokees. Repeatedly in the 18th century, when Cherokee relations with South Carolina became strained, the Cherokees would express their fear of further deterioration with the request that King George not "throw them away." In more institutionalized form, warriors on their return from war were considered ritually polluted and were kept apart for some while, as were men generally who were ill or guilty of grievous wrongdoing.

More, unfortunately, cannot be reported. Perhaps the most telling evidence is a silence in the record. There were unruly Cherokee men prone to thrust their ideas and personalities bluntly forward. Yet we read that Cherokees rarely censured one another. The presumption is reasonably strong that the curb, not easily visible to observers and perhaps not easily verbalized by Cherokees, was to withdraw.

If the ethnographic facts be assumed, it seems clear that, in the manner of Benedict, we could describe in Cherokee culture of the 1700's a consistent pattern of moral thought which disallowed face-to-face conflict. We would imagine, following her, Cherokees living through the many prehistoric generations, carrying somewhere deep in their minds an unconscious canon which guided their thoughts so that, as new situations repeatedly arose, they repeatedly made the same kind of moral choice and institutionalized those choices; over the generations, the directive to avoid conflict came finally to pervade the group life and came to be the overrriding measure of a good man.

Such a figurative reading of the moral sensibilities in Cherokee culture would not be wholly wrong, but it would lack precision. The imprecision stems not from the neglect of everyday moral imperfections in all real behavior. This study has (so far) dealt not at all with behavior, only with thoughts. But I want to characterize these Cherokee ideals more exactly. I suggest that, when viewed against the several universes of Cherokee persons operative each in its moment, such a reading of culture becomes more nearly exact, ultimately completely precise, but not in these pages. It does not seem necessary to say that there is no such thing as proper behavior except in respect to person. What behavior is regarded as decent or appropriate depends on who one is deemed to be vis-à-vis whom, in the eyes of one's fellows. This is a matter of self-evident truth, in simple societies.

The Cherokee ethos in this first meaning of the term was, then, a single, consistent pattern of thought which provided the measure of a good man. The good man dealt cautiously with his fellows, turned away to avoid threatened face-to-face conflict, and when overt conflict did occur, withdrew from the offenders. The Cherokee ethos disallowed disharmony.

CHAPTER 3

Village Councils: Ethos Again

AT THE New Year, and at other times as needed, the Cherokee village met in council and, as a single organized group, made political decisions. Cherokees required that these decisions have the appearance of unanimity. This chapter describes how such decisions were reached.

This chapter deals with role, the conduct recommended of persons. I have reported how Cherokee men imagined themselves to be properly sorted as personnel for councils, and that those many male villagers, in order to accomplish the work at hand, could make of themselves some 17 kinds of persons, as seen by a young man. I turn now to give more attention to the rules of conduct held up as appropriate for a man as one, then another, of those persons. I do not yet speak of real behavior. This chapter focuses, then, on only one structural pose, and adds roles to the description of that structure. I give attention to certain Cherokee ideas about the good man, but they are seen now as roles ascribed to persons.

The relevant facts are not readily come by in any historical record and they are but dimly reflected in the Cherokee record. I shall say that Cherokees in council tried circumspectly to work out a unanimous decision. This fact is not directly demonstrable; I shall argue its truth less directly. As before, I turn first to recent reports on contemporary Conservative Cherokee life in North Carolina and note what is briefly said there.[24] I shall turn then to the historical record and report the evidence which bears upon the same facts. This, however, would tell only part of the story. The behavior recommended in virtue of kinship connections within each clan could tell another part. Therefore, to fill that void I shall make the bald assumption, to which the historical evidence speaks not at all, that the patterns of recommended kinship behavior as reported by Gilbert in the 1930's existed also in the 1700's.[25]

The chapter has two parts. It describes the structure for village councils; to the set of persons already put down I add the corresponding roles. The chapter turns then to re-examine the Cherokee ethos seen in the context of the council and suggests a more narrow sense of the notion of ethos.

The Cherokee ethos depicts a consistent pattern of thought about decent conduct. The presumption is that that pattern of thought will be found to characterize all Cherokee activities including the village councils. We anticipate that Cherokee men, when gathered for council, thought that they should pursue their interests cautiously, avoid impending open conflict if they could, and withdraw when it occurred.

Support for this expectation is found in reports on contemporary Cherokees. One of the recurrent tasks of North Carolina Cherokee Conservatives is to arrive at group decisions. Gulick (1959:6) sums up the nature of that decision-making:

> When social decisions must be made, involving the resolution of differing points of view, the aim is circumspectly to work out a unanimous decision. An outvoted minority is regarded as a source of conflict and disharmony. Anyone whose views absolutely cannot be accommodated to the otherwise unanimous decision simply withdraws from the proceedings and is thereafter expected to "go his own way" as far as the decision is concerned. . . . The parliamentary voting procedure [usually required in official dealings with the outside] puts many Conservatives in an awkward position; they tend either to vote "for" or "yea" or to abstain altogether.

It seems clear that we deal with the Cherokee ethos: circumspection in council is the ethos recommendation of caution in pursuing one's interests generally; dropping out when one cannot accept the crystallizing group sentiment is the ethos recommendation to avoid open confrontation. Such circumspect work toward unanimity is the Cherokee ethos as expressed in group decision-making among contemporary Conservative Cherokees.

Facts from the 1700's pertaining especially to councils are very imperfectly recorded. I earlier reported that the chiefs were constrained to persuade, by "good-nature and clear reasoning, or colouring things." Timberlake reported (Williams 1927:80) that "they . . . are fond of speaking well, as that paves the way to power in their councils." Magic was used to make oneself persuasive, at councils among other places (Mooney 1900:427). Perhaps these facts weakly speak for an unusual necessity to create a common sentiment in councils. However, we are left without a single recorded clear statement as to the necessity for unanimity, in which dissenters were expected only to hold their peace and were not bound by the decision. It is virtually certain that there was no clear sense of majority decision; in the sheer quantity of Cherokee records, anything so explicit as voting would certainly have been mentioned.[26]

The one fact which was put down by nearly every observer of Cherokee life was that the chiefs were without power. Apparently that was public knowledge among non-Cherokees. South Carolina officials had perceived the absence of power in Cherokee leadership as early as 1712 (Jenkins 1949:July 9, 1712) when they sent an agent on a round of visits to some half-dozen tribes, including the Cherokee, with instructions to give the "kings" advice about:

> . . . managing Their People ye Better to keep them in Subjection, & with Example and arguments drawn from a parralell with our Government . . . [encouraging] the Cheif men . . . to maintain the authority given them by this Government.

As was mentioned above, Adair reported from his experience from 1735 on that the chiefs could "only" persuade; Johnson from experience in 1761 said there was "no such thing as coercive Power among them."

In 1757, Captain Raymond Demere, the commander of the Fort Loudoun garrison, wrote his superiors in Charles Town (Jenkins 1949:July 30, 1757):

> The [Cherokee] are an odd Kind of People, as there is no law nor Subjection amongst them. They can't be compelled to do any Thing nor oblige them to embrace any

party except they Please. The very lowest of them thinks himself as great and as high as any of the Rest . . . everyone of them must be courted for their Friendship with some kind of Feeling and made much of.

Payne (MS, IVb:66) learned from old Cherokees in the early 1800's, that, "it is by . . . native politeness alone . . . that the chiefs bind the hearts of their subjects."

Assuming these 18th century ethnographic facts, I have, as yet told little. The description so far imagines Cherokee men as a mass of villagers, unsorted as persons, and without contrasting roles. It is necessary to turn again to the universe of persons which villagers considered appropriate during councils, to ask about contrasting rules of conduct recommended to men being those several persons one to the other, and to discover thereby the web of ties through which influence might systematically move. Men came to councils with conflicting interests. No matter how circumspect Cherokees might have been, some had to yield to others. It seems also clear that the option to drop out of the proceedings could not in fact have been exercised for every casual difference. The system of persons and roles in councils is here seen as a kind of tool which, when used, caused influence to flow in nonrandom ways and which provided some measure of assurance that villages would successfully reconcile interests, for most members, most of the time.

For councils, the village considered it appropriate to be organized in seven clans and in an overall body of elders. (I use "clan" in this context in place of the more cumbersome "clan section," to mean that section of the tribal-wide clan residing in one village.) In decision-making these two structures functioned approximately as follows: each clan attempted to reach a corporate opinion. The older men from the seven clans (the beloved men) then joined the village priestly officials and became for the moment the body of elders. They talked over the sentiments of their various clans. Then these beloved men talked again with their own respective clans, reporting opinions of the other clans, then gathered again as elders, and so on. Probably both sets of discussions included public speeches; a general council probably gave the outward appearance of a New England town meeting, with un-New England-like caucuses going on intermittently. Councils continued in this loose manner for days or, with interruptions, for weeks.

The first phase of decision-making occurred within each of the corporate clan sections. There each adult man was to each other man one of eight kinds of persons, as shown earlier—mother's brother, nephew, older brother, younger brother, clan brother, beloved mother's brother, beloved older brother, beloved clan brother. For each of these persons, there was a role. Although there were some contrasts among the roles of younger brother, older brother, or fictive clan brother, these appear to have been of minor consequence in the context of councils; they may therefore be lumped and termed simply brother. Thus, every man was, with every other, one of two sets of kin:

brother-with-brother
mother's brother-with-nephew

The role behavior attached to these persons seems to have made of them available tools of considerable effectiveness for each clan to accomplish the immediate task at hand, to arrive at a corporate clan sentiment.

Brothers (young and old and fictive) had the right morally to censure one another. To accomplish this, brothers had license to "tease and threaten a large number of practical jokes which are calculated to make the offender uncomfortable for the rest of his life."[27] However, some brothers were beloved men, and some not; toward beloved men deference was generally due. The presumption is strong that during councils such moral censuring could be exercised primarily by beloved men against brothers who were young men, and among brothers who were age-mates, old or young, but not by young men against brothers who were beloved men.

Similarly, a mother's brother was disciplinarian over his growing nephew. As the nephew matured, the mother's brother seems not to have continued that direct disciplinary power, but he could command unusual respect and was privileged mildly to joke with his nephew. Mother's brothers were typically a generation older than their nephews; very often, among adults, the mother's brother would be a beloved man, his nephew a young man.

We find, then, within each clan a set of persons and roles which, if used, become a channel of strong influence, causing that influence to flow from old to young. The clans had legitimate powers of coercion. Young men entered councils vulnerable; their older fellow clansmen held weapons which could induce young men to defer.

The older members of a clan were to each other brothers and occasionally mother's brothers, and nephews. Among these age-mates within a clan there was the same license of mutual censuring and joking, according to kin connection. Among these older clansmen, kinship roles were again potential tools. These tools could not help resolve a stalemate in which men were divided into approximately equal camps; the potential duress between pairs of brothers would simply be canceled out, and it does not seem likely that one camp would happen to include more mother's brothers to press the other camp's nephews. These kinship roles could, however, if used, cause one or a very few old men to knuckle under to the crystallized sentiment of most of his age mates in the clan.

These persons and roles, then, within each clan seem to have provided machinery by which each clan could often and with some disciplined speed arrive at a single corporate opinion. This would end the first phase of decision-making.

So far we have not described that circumspect behavior which presumably characterized 18th century Cherokee councils. But it seemed permissible at the beginning of this chaper to infer such behavior from the evidence of contemporary Cherokee decision-making and the historical record. The apparent contradiction between these rather harsh sanctions and my earlier assumption is easily cleared up. A Cherokee could act harshly in one role but would not have to act similarly in a different role.

I mention again some of the historical reports: Cherokees "seldom turn their eyes on the person they speak of, or address themselves to"; they "seldom contradict or censure one another." This does not appear to describe the expected relations among brothers or between mother's brothers and nephews. We read that chiefs were without power, that they could only "persuade," that they exercised "native politeness alone." This does not appear to describe the expected behavior of old toward young inside the clans.

I suggest that these descriptions apply to the expectations of proper behavior among elders in council. These data, then, must be read: a man, as elder, seldom turns his eyes on other elders whom he addresses (while the same man may glower at a younger brother needing moral censuring); elders seldom contradict one another; elders have no power over elders, etc.

A second phase of decision-making occurred within the body of elders; within this body, under the leadership of the priest-officials, the beloved men from the seven clans faced the task of reconciling the various sentiments of the corporate clans.

The young men were quite outside these second deliberations. Young men were expected to demonstrate deference toward the priests. Priests, in turn, were expected sometimes mildly to scold for unruly conduct (Payne MS, IVb:68). However, such occasions of direct relationship between young men and priests seem to have been infrequent. The relations of young men to the priestly officials were mediated through the beloved men of the respective clans. Similarly, young men had no direct relations with the beloved men of other clans; they were expected, however, to show deference to age. A young man was expected not to intrude on the remaining members of the other clans, that is, the young men of the village. The young men had no important part in the reconciliation of clan sentiments. It follows that the persons and roles among the old men, acting as elders, were the tools upon which rested the chances of success in this aspect of decision-making.

Any elder might have numerous grandfathers among the elders of other clans (all men from the clans of his mother's father and father's father), i.e., he would be grandson to those individuals. These grandfathers were privileged to tease mildly, but it is not clear that such teasing could be made to have coercive bite. Any elder might have fathers (the men from his own father's clan) among the elders. These men would probably enjoy sufficient respect to affect the flow of influence within the body of elders. And, of course, each man might be also grandfather and father to others among the elders.

But these kinship relations could not systematically assist the reconciliation of clan sentiments, because it was not assured that any one clan would be in a vulnerable position in respect to another. Marriage preference rules appear to have been but mildly recommended, and would not, in any event, have caused the members of one clan to be predominantly grandsons or sons and therefore vulnerable to members of another clan. Kinship roles among elders did not assist very much the deliberations in the body of elders.

The chances of success depended, rather, on a common denominator of the several roles expected of elders in their relations within that body. (There were minor contrasts of recommended behavior within that body, corresponding to the various persons there; for example, contrasts between appropriate conduct toward clan spokesmen and toward other elders; but the record does not reveal much.) Put otherwise, the several roles attached to the several persons among the elders held up as appropriate that same set of recommended conduct we discovered in the attempt to describe the Cherokee ethos.[28]

Elders were expected to reconcile contrasting clan sentiments by pursuing cautiously the interests of their respective clans, avoiding direct conflict through judicious compromise and maneuverings whenever possible, and allowing elders to drop out if that became unavoidable. Effectiveness among the elders would indeed appear to require "good nature and clear reasoning, or colouring things" and would be facilitated by "native politeness." One can also easily imagine that a conjurer with a "persuasive" medicine would find customers.

It is apparent that the role of an elder in council differed from the kinship role within the clan. The effective use of this role was an art to be acquired through continued application; the elders would not be equally proficient in this art. Success depended on their practiced capacity to sense quickly and accurately the thoughts of others, and to reveal their own thoughts, first with calculated ambiguity, then cautiously and convincingly to reveal those thoughts more narrowly, finally to state the matter exactly, in a manner which brought group sentiment to a final crystallization.

It must be assumed that the elders of a clan who strongly objected to sentiment as it became crystallized among the remaining elders were expected to hold their peace; if they failed to do so then the villagers began to avoid them. A clan whose elders dropped out was not bound by the council decision.

The two phases of decision-making were not clearly separated. An observer could not easily have identified particular actions with either phase. The unanimity which might emerge was not unanimity of eager assent.

The major outlines of a Cherokee village in one of its orderings is now apparent.

I would like to emphasize that the foregoing description is in terms of social structure. Social structure implies enduring ideas, persons and roles; here they may be regarded as a set of devices facilitating the making of decisions. This set was available to all Cherokees of a village, but how many Cherokees used the devices is another question. Still another question is how effectively they used it. Behavior has not yet been described.

I turn now to consider the Cherokee ethos, this time in the context of the set of persons and roles available for councils. The roles during councils were much less uniform than prescribed by the Cherokee ethos. In delineating ethos we employed the words: caution, circumspection. In the description of councils we used those same words but in addition: scolding, duress, censure.

The notion of structural pose sorts Cherokee persons and roles into the four sets in which they were actually made available for work. Those four structural poses were available recurrently through the year to accomplish a series of male tasks. I have used the notion of ethos in an effort to order facts which are pervasive in Cherokee life in such a way as to give understanding of Cherokee culture through calling attention to few, but significant facts. My description of the Cherokee ethos should say something that is true of each structural pose if the characterization it provides is to be useful in the understanding of Cherokee culture.

The Cherokee ethos, seen as a consistent pattern of thought disallowing conflict, has not yet been fully described. We have now before us only one structural pose, that set of persons available for councils, and have yet to look at ethos in the context of other poses. But even within this one pose there is a heterogeneity of role which is not clearly reconciled with the Cherokee ethos as described. It is not enough simply to report that. Benedict tells us that ethos does or does not, in any particular case, penetrate equally all culture (all roles); she reports an interesting fact, but it is not very enlightening. I seek further to discover whether some more narrowed and more useful meaning of ethos does not recommend itself. I examine three meanings of ethos in the light of the heterogeneity of recommended conduct during Cherokee councils. The question is: In what more exact sense can the Cherokee ethos be said to characterize the village council?

The reported Cherokee pattern of moral thought could have the meaning that circumspect caution was more often the recommended conduct than other rules of appropriateness and decency. Guided by that meaning, one would make a check-list of every kind of person a Cherokee man might be vis-à-vis all others; one would weight each of those persons according to the greater or less number of individuals who in fact were expected to be each one. Then one would list the set of corresponding roles. This analysis would only suggest that caution was a feature of the roles most frequently recommended. It is very doubtful that mere frequency was the phenomenon which impressed Benedict or other students of group life, and caused them intuitively to grasp the patterns which they have reported as ethos.

Caution, including minding one's own business, seems to have been the most frequent operating role during councils; this was true, largely because young men were "other clansman" to the members of six of the seven clans, and it was thought to be proper that young men not intrude in the affairs of other clansmen during councils. But that bears only on the fact that the clans arrived severally at corporate decisions, which fact reveals very little about the council and could, in any event, be found out more economically. This meaning of ethos is put aside.

There remain two other meanings suggested by the description of the Cherokee council. One was ethnographically true; the other may or may not have been true; both are significant facts to know about a people.

This next possible meaning cannot be established as true or false from the Cherokee record. This meaning permits us to imagine that, in virtue of the reported consistent pattern of thought, Cherokee roles with all their contrasts had yet a single coloration. We read that Cherokee brothers could morally censure one another; but we do not read whether they were enjoined to leap at every slight opportunity to do so or to do so reluctantly, after exhausting less coercive measures, as a final necessity. Nor do we read how mother's brothers went about demanding the respect properly due them; whether such demands were made often or rarely, with public bluster or discretely. So we do not know to what degree these stressful relations depart from others more circumspect.

Consideration of the possibility of a single coloration of roles serves merely to remind that anthropologists put down only the grossest facts about role and have not yet learned to observe important details, even in studies which especially focus on social structure. We virtually never know whether it is recommended that an individual, as some person, speak loud or soft, fast or slow; that he hold his body tense or relaxed; that his eyes be darting about seeking the eyes of his audience, or focused off in space, etc., etc. Such facts about role which need reporting for structural studies are not subtle, though they are assumed to be and are sometimes termed minimal cues. They are public markers, publicly significant behavior speaking loudly to the actors who respond in terms of approval or disapproval. If the actors can see, so can we. We need, in order to describe social structures, to record only those actions which are recognized as publicly meaningful to the actors, but we need all such actions.[29] Now, it seems, though no one states it explicitly, that our curiosity about social structure is satisfied when we have identified persons. We report without apology descriptions of corresponding roles, but these gross reported facts are really by-products of our work—they are the facts, i.e., rights and obligations and other gross markers, which happen to have been recorded by the time we feel secure in the identification of a new person; at that moment we proceed to look elsewhere. Paradoxically, without a much fuller set of role facts, we cannot even discover all the persons used by a group.

A third meaning in the notion of ethos is suggested by the lack of uniformity among Cherokee roles during councils. In this meaning, ethos may be taken to depict that part of a people's pattern of moral thought which recommends the striving to achieve unusual excellence, a moral virtuosity in human relations (according to the group's selected rules), an achievement to be sought and, if reached, rewarded. The good man is an unusual and an honored man. A people may expect moral virtuosity in some class, or clan, or age-group and, within such groups, unevenly among the members. Some notion about moral virtuosity appears to be a human universal. In the Cherokee instance, it seems clear that young men (men younger than about 55) were simply not expected, as a body, to exhibit this quality in a dependably consistent manner. Hence, in the Cherokee case, the goal held up was a lifetime goal, to be achieved in whatever degree possible in one's later years. The record is reasonably clear that events in Cherokee life (for example the major ceremonies) demonstrated and emphasized that being a good elder—and especially a priest—was the highest possible achievement. Being effectively an elder, or becoming a priest, appears to have required some large measure of this moral virtuosity. The capacity for circumspect relations, honor, and influence—these qualities of an elder were to be achieved in a lifetime. Among the old men, achievement was expected to vary; but leaders within that body were expected to come close to the ideal.

Ethos in this meaning is a measure of decent conduct; it is held up as an ideal to all; but conformity to the ideal is not expected within some sections of the society; performance consistent with the ethos is expected of members in other sections but in varying degrees, for moral virtuosity is expected to be rare.

The last two meanings discussed lead to useful inquiries. We ought to know whether diverse roles in one society take on a single coloration different from the colorations of similar roles in another society. We ought to know also a society's notions about moral virtuosity. The two kinds of inquiry deserve distinct names. "Ethos" seems to fit most comfortably the meaning which suggests the last sort of inquiry.

Benedict's phrase, "singleness of purpose," meant many things to her, but it fits well this last meaning. I now say, more narrowly than before, that the Cherokee ethos was a consistent pattern of thought which held up a standard of circumspect, harmonious conduct, and recommended achievement of moral virtuosity under that standard as the overriding moral purpose of a Cherokee lifetime. The essential measure of a good man was the ability to maintain cautious, quiet relations, avoiding clashes of interest; men were expected to honor others who, by that measure, were good, and were expected to hope that they might approximate that goal, as an ultimate achievement in their later years.

So defined, ethos asserts something true and significant about the total set of roles available during councils. Moral virtuosity was a lifetime goal and old men were expected to approximate that conduct. Defined this way, the conception of Cherokee ethos leaves no inscrutable "exceptions" to explain. Harmony was to Cherokees a measure of moral excellence, but Cherokees did not expect young men to achieve that excellence and used forms of decent duress toward and among young men to get necessary work done. There is no reason to suppose Cherokees felt this incongruous.

So defined, ethos seems to assert important truth about any structural pose. In the Cherokee case, moral excellence was possible only in one's later years, hence old and young were the large contrasting sections of Cherokee society. Among structural poses, the implications vary. In the Cherokee case, the central fact to watch is the combinations of old and young which each pose drew together.

This chapter described the Cherokee council as a set of persons and roles which, if brought effectively into use, caused influence to move in nonrandom ways. Within each clan section kinship roles could force young to yield to old and thereby permit the seven clans to develop corporate sentiments. To the old men as elders fell the task of reconciling the clan sentiments so that the village could arrive at a single sentiment having the appearance of unanimity; the roles among elders were shown to recommend the same conduct seen earlier as the Cherokee ethos.

In Chapter 2, I presented an approximation of the Cherokee ethos which held up the ability to avoid conflict as the measure of a good man. This chapter reviewed recommended behavior in councils and found these roles less uniform than the ethos as described would indicate. In that light I examined three possible meanings of ethos and chose one—ethos is a measure of moral virtuosity; it is held up as ideal to all; performance by that standard is not expected within some sections of society; performance is expected in other sections but in varying degrees. The good man is expectably a rare man.

In seeking this first characterization of Cherokee ethos I let go of person, as is usually done in ethos studies. If one lets go of person, one must be content with figurative language and approximate meaning. In simple societies, ideas about right conduct vary according to persons. A statement of ethos ought to assert something true about role heterogeneity in each of the actual sets of persons and roles which a people are recommended to be and act.

In the Cherokee instance the narrow meaning of ethos put in focus young and old as contrasting sections of Cherokee society. The Cherokee ethos could be stated as an overriding lifetime moral purpose. This meaning adds to the understanding of all the persons-with-roles which were available during Cherokee village councils. For example, the phrase young man comes now to mean not-yet-man, and the roles of young men come to be conduct expected of the morally immature.

CHAPTER 4

War Organization

ALL Cherokee policy was made in council. That policy was variously implemented.

About the administration of certain areas of policy, nothing can be said. We cannot describe the construction and repair of public buildings nor the collective aspects of agricultural work; the record does not permit.

This chapter focuses on the implementation of policy decisions in foreign affairs. We view the village war organization as a system of authority: unlike councils which were systems of influence, war behavior was coordinated through the exercise and threat of physical coercion.

In carrying on offensive war, the village implemented some of its more difficult decisions. When a council decided for war, the Cherokee village could become an order of command for war: The war organization could form itself and become the major actor; the body of elders would nominally remain an actor. The war organization was equipped to implement the group decision for war through a chain of command created in some part by the offices and ranks of that organization. However, this set of offices and ranks was rarely used in its totality. When one views the war organization as a universe of persons and roles, it reveals itself as a complex mass which, as persons and roles, was not workable.

This chapter does not in the main describe persons and roles; they appear not to have much affected the actions of warriors. Rather it reports observations which seem to reflect real and highly variable behavior among warriors. The behavior is merely reported, and I shall assert that that behavior was importantly acultural.

The chapter has two parts. I characterize the behavior of the warriors. I then briefly apply the notion of ethos for the light it casts on these war relations.

The village, especially at the annual New Year council in September, had to decide on peace or war with any of a host of foreign powers. With the new year came winter, and winter in the Southeast was the season of warfare. To the village at any time, some of the alien tribes and colonial powers were not clearly friends or clearly enemies. Many young men were eager to seek titles and prestige on the warpath. Against what tribe should they go? The council under the village priest chief decided for or against war.[30] When a decision for war or peace became a council issue, certain foremost war officials—probably those older priests for war, the war priest, the war chief, the war speaker, and the surgeon—spoke in their official war capacities. (When other matters were being decided, they sat, undifferentiated, in the body of elders.) If peaceful actions by a foreign power seemed probable, the village council might forbid raids; if attacks seemed probable, the village might allow the young men to attack first; and if the intentions of a power were imponderable, the village might send out a party of young men to negotiate.

During these deliberations of the council, the young men participated as in any councils, that is, as members of their several clan sections. If the decision was for war, the members of the age status young man soon formed the war organization. At home, during councils, young men acted as members of their several clans; away from home, during offensive war, young men acted as members of the war organization. The alternation of these two sets of persons occurred as the seasons for war came and went. I shall reserve the word warrior to denote young males forming the war organization, and the term young man to denote them at home.

The influence of the body of elders affecting warriors on the warpath was purely nominal; the elders could not consistently know about nor reliably control the actions of war parties, once the warriors were outside the village. If old enemies should propose friendship, or old friends commit hostilities, the elders were usually unable to affect the behavior of war parties until they returned to the village. When they returned, the village could resume its structure for councils, and earlier decisions could be changed. Here again, the young males participated in the decisions, but as young men, not as warriors. If war was newly decided, the young men became again warriors and formed the war organization. Similarly, and for the same reasons, actions by clan sections affecting parties on the warpath were largely nominal in their influence; however, these clans had representatives on the seven-man war council inside the war organization; so each clan had its interests represented, for example, in respect to clan revenge.

Hence, the essential relations for implementing policy in respect to war and peace were the relations among warriors inside the war organization. Cherokee villages usually had over 100 warriors. After a council decision for war, and after ritual preparations, the war party left the village in a formal procession according to the offices and ranks of the war organization. The formal social machinery of the war organization was elaborate. In the event of surprise in the field, the war speaker was expected to give the orders; in the event of planned attack, the war chief. Scouts were sent out ahead, to the right and left, and behind, chosen according to their several war ranks. The war priest or his stand-in was asked about when and how to attack. One preferred strategy was to set V-shaped ambush, using a few warriors as lures. Or, if a direct attack on an enemy camp was required, the preferred strategy was to attack in two wings. Before such an attack on an enemy camp, the war speaker was expected to make a fiery speech; then, the war chief, standard bearer, and speaker were expected to go straight to the first house of the enemy and not to retreat until victorious or dead or unless dragged back by the warriors; analogous behavior was expected of the seven war councilmen (Payne MS, IVb:171).

By the first new moon of the Cherokee summer, war parties returned. On their return to the village, warriors had to pass through a ritual purification (Payne MS, III:79–80). With that rite the war organization disbanded. A warrior who had distinguished himself was given a war title by the village, and people would hoe his corn field to honor him.

However, as was stated in Chapter 1, the formal war machinery appears to have been cumbersome beyond utility as a result of the mere number of possible persons the various members could be one to the other. Essentially, this was because the whole web of kinship connections was present in addition to the large set of offices and ranks of the organization. Both were considered operative and varied independently of one another. As stated before, the potential number of operative persons was about 250.[31] Such complexity appears to have offered no means for an orderly handling of authority.

A strong indication that authority did not flow through some system of persons and roles is the inconsistency in recorded observations about warriors. Some White observers assert that there was no legitimate compulsion by war leaders over members of war parties, that leaders had to rely on inspiring their men to great voluntary effort. In the 1760's, Timberlake (Williams 1927:93) reported that the Cherokee war leaders

. . . lead the warriors that choose to go, for there is no law of compulsion on those that refuse to follow, or punishment to those that forsake their chief. . . .

Adair (1775:381), speaking of the southeastern tribes, said of warriors that:

. . . if their dreams portend any will, they always obey the supposed divine intimation and return home, without incurring the least censure. They reason that their readiness to serve their country, should not be subservient to their own knowledge or wishes, but always regulated by the divine impulse. I have known a whole company who set out for war, to return in small parties, and sometimes by single persons, and be applauded by the united voices of the people. . . .

Timberlake (Williams 1927:93) adds that war leaders relied on inspiring their men:

[The war leader] strives therefore, to inspire them with a sort of enthusiasm, by the war song, as the ancient bards did once in Britain.

Similarly, Adair (1775:378):

[War leaders] are fully satisfied, if they have revenged crying blood, enobled themselves by war actions, given cheerfulness to their mourning country, and fired the breasts of the youth with a spirit of emulation to guard the beloved people from danger, and revenge the wrongs of the country. Warriors are to protect all, but not to molest the meanest.[32]

Sometimes the Cherokees themselves, both early and late in the period under consideration, testified that the relations among warriors were not properly coercive. In 1725, a Cherokee war leader, King Crow, said that the warriors might "promise to go to war (but it's when they please)" (Willis 1955:190).

And in 1757, Great Warrior (Aganstata) of Echota, one of the foremost warriors in Cherokee history, wrote Demere asking that Demere be lenient toward some English soldiers who had deserted and were returning. Aganstata revealed the self-image of a kindly protector rather than a stern disciplinarian when he wrote (Jenkins 1949: April 5, 1757):

we Warriors that carry People and have People under our Charge we love these People so I hope you forgive them this one Fault. I am very Glad to see them come back, For we Warriours when we are at War, if we lose a Man, we are uneasy and when he comes back we are very glad, so [I] hope that you will be glad likewise. . . .

There exists a recorded brief glimpse of actual war behavior which seems to confirm the above reports. In 1766, there was an instance apparently recounted by a participant. A war party under one Tiftoe was surprised in their camp. Most of the warriors fled but Tiftoe "animated them by a strong and bold speech, throwing off all his cloathes, & killing the [enemy] Head Warrior on the first onset. . . ." The party rallied and beat off the enemy (Saunders 1886–90, VII: 209–10).

In spite of the above reports, the presence of a measure of actual coercive authority among warriors is suggested by a fact apparent repeatedly in the earliest records. The war organization was the segment of the village which could be manipulated by outsiders. It would serve a trader little immediate purpose to make suggestions as to actions by a village to a beloved man, irrespective of how trustful his personal relations with the beloved man might be. The beloved man, if he acted according to Cherokee expectations, would take the idea to his fellow elders and there would follow the interminable discussions characteristic of the body of elders. With a leading warrior it was apparently different. A war leader could be induced to act; through some disciplined order of command, his own followers could join him in immediate action. In 1714, three English traders were able to manipulate a few war leaders in such manner. The result was the destruction of a Yuchi town nearby which was in debt to the traders. (The warriors paid the Yuchi debts with part of the loot.) In 1742, Antoine Bonnefoy reported (Williams 1928: 158) that English traders were similarly manipulating the war organizations by forming their own war parties among the Cherokees—through war leaders, calling parties together, outfitting them, and sending them against tribes which were in the French interest.

Further, in spite of the apparent notion among White observers and Cherokee villagers that war relations were not properly coercive, other descriptions indicate that authoritarian behavior was recommended conduct for the war leaders toward their followers. One Buttrick informant (Payne MS, III: 15) made the observation that war leaders exercised very great authority. This informant said that:

. . . warriors were under very strict rules: and one by disobeying, and committing sin, caused God to leave them, so that they could not destroy their enemies. This man however was condemned to die.

Apparently certain persons and roles were vehicles for the legitimate exercise of authority. The person war chief appears to have carried an authoritarian role. Buttrick's informants described the inauguration of a new war chief (Payne MS, III:65–68). The retiring chief, they said, directed the inauguration and instructed the young men to obey the new chief and never go to war without his permission. The new war chief made an acceptance speech:

You have now put me in blood to my knees. . . . You have made me *a ska yi gu stu e go* and I shall endeavour to take care of my young warriors, and never expose them in war unnecessarily.

Then the civil priests and the war priests filed past the new war chief and called him "mother's brother." The mother's brother was the disciplinarian of the Cherokee family. The exercise of certain circumscribed authority over warriors was explicitly provided by the set of war offices listed above; these necessary directive functions in a war party were assigned to members of the party according to traditional criteria. Adair, speaking of southeastern tribes generally, reported (1775:382):

Every war captain chooses a noted warrior, to attend him and the company. . . . Everything they eat or drink during the journey, he gives them out of his hand. . . .

All of these seem to involve persons and roles—fully legitimate usages.

We saw in Chapter 1 the appearance of disutility in the very quantity of possible war persons. We have seen assertions that there was no allowed coercive authority among warriors, and other indirect indications that there was some actual authority; there are also some reports of a few particular war persons with legitimately coercive roles. These records seem to me to permit the inference that actual war behavior was unusually diverse, and that Cherokee war work was incompletely and imperfectly institutionalized. The relations within war parties were, I believe, not much ordered by social structure; war behavior was (in that sense only) acultural. Warriors at war were controlled, but not through the devices of persons and roles in any significant measure.

I do not say that war behavior was random—no real behavior is that. I shall say in Chapter 5 that it was not random in respect to personality, that the very lack of control during war gave free rein to different personalities, and some kinds of men came to the top as war leaders.

Under the same structure as for offensive war, the village carried on foreign negotiations. A certain lack of control in the interrelations of the young men sent out as negotiators was frequently recorded. As early as 1717, a young Cherokee behaved insolently toward his fellows during negotiations with South Carolina; other members of the party beat him in turn (Jenkins 1949:May 9, 1717). In the late 1750's and afterwards, a Cherokee with a growing reputation for skill in negotiations was usually called by observers "testy," "vain," "conceited," etc., toward both aliens and fellow Cherokees (Logan 1859:487–90).

There is, of course, the possibility that the historical records leave inadequate materials, or that the materials have been wrongly read. Perhaps there was greater structural order among war parties than here reported. I can but note two facts: that, in sheer quantity, the records of war and foreign negotiations are much greater than those bearing on councils (the Cherokee historical record was put down, primarily, by colonial officials who had more frequent contact with warriors than with elders), and that the records on councils did, ultimately, fall into order while the records on war did not. However, in respect to councils, contemporary professional observations by Thomas and Gulick and by Gilbert could be brought to bear; no corresponding contemporary observations facilitate the interpretation of war matters.

I make, then, an assumption as to ethnographic fact: Cherokee war work was incompletely and imperfectly institutionalized. Perhaps the evidence cited lends some credence to that assumption.

Human societies tend to be moral orders, and simple human societies tend to be so pervasively, as Redfield (1953) and others have noted. There is a strong tendency, when circumstances permit societies a measure of stability, to attach to patterned relationships moral significance. To describe social structure (as conceived here) is to describe moral sentiments about relations among men, to put all such sentiments in systematic relation one to the other, and thereby to characterize a human community in one of its revealing aspects.

In a simple and stable human community such as a Cherokee village, most of group life is ordered by moral sentiments. In such a social order, the recurrent presence of relations not ordered by notions about decency is, I must suppose, a source of some measure of uneasiness. Cherokees would perceive such behavior as un-Cherokee. It would produce discomfort because it could not be handled in the accustomed manner.

If this be so, one other ethnographic fact supports the assertion that war relations were not much controlled by moral sentiments—by person and role. Perhaps Cherokee discomfort is revealed by a negative attitude toward war among Cherokees in terms of their larger valuings. In Cherokee minds, war was simply less natural than peace. Adair (1775:388), speaking of southeastern tribes generally, said:

[They hold] that man was not born in a state of war; and as they reckon they are become impure by shedding human blood, they hasten to observe the fast of three days . . . and be sanctified. . . .

War was referred to in terms which, to Western observers at least, connoted negative feelings: when hostilities broke out, the path became dark, dirty, bloody (Jenkins 1949:March 27, 1757 and June 13, 1757).

I suggest that the Cherokee ethos as here understood helps characterize the war organization. The notion of ethos also points toward a possible solution of an inherent puzzle concerning the war organization: that is, the absence of an adequate system of persons and roles available for the orderly performance of recurrent tasks.

If we think of ethos in the earlier meaning of Chapter 2, we would consider the relations among warriors as exceptions to the ethos, or perhaps we would attempt to locate a second focus of Cherokee values. In its narrowed meaning, however, ethos brought into relief the fact that Cherokees thought of achieving decency as a lifetime purpose. The central feature of the structural pose for war is that it separated young from old, making the young men virtually autonomous during the execution of certain war policies. The ethos enjoined that those autonomous young men were not-yet-men, a fact of some importance in describing warriors at war. As with the situation of young men in councils, we deal here with Cherokee expectations of the morally immature; but in contrast to their situation in councils, the young men were not under systematic duress through their kinship relations.

The Cherokee ethos held that old equals decent, and, as we might put it, that boys will be boys (until 55). If warriors were so defined, elders could shrug off the violation of council directives by war parties. The social cost was usually not great, and the warriors themselves might revel in the irresponsibility assigned them.

I have suggested that, if the description of ethos be regarded as depicting a people's ideas about moral virtuosity, knowing the ethos helps in the description of the observable behavior in classes, age-groups, or other social sections which are expected to be morally inept. We deal, of course, with learned behavior, with taught self-images, with a kind of learning which is not usually reported for simple societies; here is a section of a population learning to be "bad." A wider meaning of ethos does not illumine such facts.

Knowledge of the Cherokee ethos, as now understood, seems also to help explain why war work was imperfectly institutionalized. The village war work was crisis work and therefore different in an important way from the work of the councils. In councils the large decisions affecting the village were made. Decision-making in councils moved slowly; leisurely discussions continued for days, even weeks. Typically, councils could take their time. In war, there was no time to lose. The slow nurturing of consensus was less important than the quick coordination of action. Without time for discussion and with, often, the survival of the war party depending on the correct action from every individual, coercion was functional.

Coercion need not, however, be ordered by social structure. The record suggests some measure of de facto coercion. From the standpoint of the survival needs of the war parties, it is not possible to say that more coercion, or coercion more ordered by social structure, was functionally necessary.

From the standpoint of the needs of the village at large, it appears that only authority ordered by social structure would be dependably responsive to council directives. However, Cherokee villages traditionally, and into the early 1700's, could afford some structural inadequacy in this section of their political system. The degree of institutionalization already apparent, plus the overall appearance of the war organization as some dreamed-up and perhaps hoped-for structure for command, perhaps indicate some mildly felt need. But war among tribes was as much a sport as serious business. Wars were rarely instruments used by design to gain territory, although de facto boundaries shifted according to relatively long-term trends in the fortunes of war. Thus, there was no pressing need for greater institutionalization of war work.[33]

In the absence of a pressing need, Cherokee thoughts about moral virtuosity would perhaps check any tendency to further institutionalization of war activities. The Cherokee ethos held that the highest decency was circumspect relations—clearly not the commandeering relations useful in war. In terms of such an ethos, old and young might expectably find it especially difficult to devise fully legitimate authority relations among warriors.

I have suggested that the interrelations among warriors were in some large measure acultural in that they were not much ordered by social structure. The formal structure which nominally existed seems not to have provided a set of persons and roles which were workable as tools for channeling authority for the war work. The warriors were controlled, but not by social structure.

I further pointed out two implications of ethos, as now understood, in this structural pose: the Cherokee ethos helps characterize the relations among warriors and possibly helps explain why war work was not ordered in important ways by persons and roles.

CHAPTER 5

A Bridge to the Individual

THIS chapter goes a small distance toward understanding Cherokee behavior in 18th century village politics. Up to this point we have looked at structures for politics; I now look for patterns of political behavior. I consider first the apparent limits of the contribution which social structure itself can make to understanding human behavior; the obvious necessity, on the other hand, of including structural facts in attempts to understand human action; and the bridge built by the notion of structural pose between facts of social structure and facts of human experience, hence to real behavior. Second, I attempt to discover in the recurrent experience of Cherokee young men and old men, taken as two blocs of men, the sources of predispositions they might share to take up the persons and roles provided for political work. Finally, I consider selected Cherokee life careers and attempt to discover indications of Cherokee personality types which moved through the village political system, that is, I seek variations in the predispositions among Cherokees to take up those recommended persons and roles.

Cultural anthropologists are students of behavior; as cultural anthropologists we have special interests in social persistence and change, and in the wide but bounded potentialities of human nature. If we are soon given important new knowledge in those directions, such knowledge will largely come from students of the field called personality and culture and from others heavily indebted to them. This brief chapter looks toward their realm, the notion of the human individual.

The study of social structure draws from part of behavior, that which is done with an eye to an audience. It looks at actions and at approving and disapproving reactions and learns thereby a people's value thoughts, termed here persons and roles; those thoughts, put in order, depict a social structure. These are crucial facts to know, and virtually nothing interesting in human behavior is knowable without them. But such ordered facts, by themselves, tell us about valuings, not about behavior.

From a described social structure, it is possible to know that a people imagine that a certain person and a corresponding role exist. From some descriptions of social structure it is often possible to know the occasions when the people usually recommend that some of themselves be that person. With such knowledge some behavior can be predicted; *if* the people on a particular occasion in fact do recommend to some one man this person, *if* he accepts it, and *if* he behaves accordingly, *then* the people will feel or express approval. But these are the data summed up by the description, so that nothing new is added. Described social structure seems unable to handle any of those "ifs" except spuriously by the common, implicit assumption that most of the people most of the time will act in the usual and recommended ways.[31] Precisely these questions about real behavior are the central issue in one of the two larger anthropological interests—in all problems of social persistence and change. Probably, the growing tip of social change is always some reduction in the frequency with which people act in the recommended manner.

The effort in studies of social structure has not been spent at that level, but in attempting to discover covariation among structural items, that is, to establish types of structures. This search follows the other large anthropological interest—the wide but bounded limits of the human potential. However, the report that a people have a Crow kinship system and also matrilineal clans sweeps those same imponderables out of sight; clearly, the strength of covariation among these facts depends upon unanswered questions about real behavior, since a people can combine any structural idea with any other if they do not often act in the ways implied. One has the strong sense that the search for types is endless on this equivocal basis.

Due caution recommends, then, some pessimism as to the potential scholarly use of social structure taken alone, beyond ordered description of selected fact.

To understand is correctly to predict.[35] Prediction about social persistence and change and about the limited forms of human variability seems impossible until we can say among other things that a man will accept his person and role under certain conditions and will not under others.

To understand real behavior requires that facts be ordered in terms of the notion of individual. So far this study has been based on the notion of the person; we have dealt with enduring thoughts publicly shared by all men in a society. A person is no one man, nor is any man but one person. In contrast, the notion of individual depicts organisms which are born, live, and die. The notion of individual orders facts with an eye to the organism which experiences and with an eye to the sequence of that experience. One man's experience may be the focus of inquiry, or many men sharing some common sets of experience. In either event, the student sets out, in effect, to "follow that man."

There is a crucial difference between the notion of individual and the notion of person. The notion of person is timeless. To elicit the Cherokee ethos, it made no difference whether each appearance of the structural pose for council came before or after the pose for war, whether in each instance these two were juxtaposed or separated in time, or whether in a given year the total duration of one was the same, or greater, or less than that of the other. As so far studied, all occurrences of the pose for council were noted and studied together as were all instances of the pose for war, at no cost to the analysis of structure or ethos. The notion of individual, if it is to do different work, may not be timeless. The utility of the idea derives from the fact that the notion is geared to experiencing organisms and, usually, the sequence and duration of experience are judged to be crucial data. One man may be under scrutiny or a whole society, but if data are ordered according to duration and sequence of experiences, the study moves on the axis of the individual.

It seems evident: through analyzing experiencing men, one by one or en masse, we may hope to arrive at some comprehension of predispositions which cause those men, for example, to take up or not take up recommended persons and roles. This procedure might move us toward understanding behavior; toward predictive knowledge about social systems.

Social structure cannot account for behavior; to do so we must consider the experiencing men, and experience is approached through the notion of individual. But it is a related and obvious point that, among the kinds of fact which must be known about experiencing humans, social structure is one of great importance. Men act at some moment. They bring to that moment their life experience; they are, at that moment, in a certain environment. Social structure is an important part of this life experience and of this environment.

To understand a man's internalized career at any point in time—his personality—students of personality would seem to need the facts called social structure. Such students tell us that an overriding fact of the human is that it symbolizes; among the symbols that the human mind entertains, none enters behavior more persistently than the persons one has imagined himself to be, and has been imagined to be (together with the corresponding roles). A lifetime is, among other things, a constant movement into and out of persons-with-roles. A human personality carries with it this experience. The result of the experience, at a given moment, is some fund of psychic energy ready to find some expression.

The second important fact about man is that he stands at any moment of action in an environment. One feature of the environment is that it includes a social structure. A man knows that others know that on this occasion a certain set of persons-and-roles is appropriate. Such a milieu may stimulate or inhibit expression.

So social structure is two things: it is a large dimension of men's life experience, incorporated in their personalities; and it is a large dimension of the environment in the moment at which men act.

Studies of social structure, I said, take raw structural facts and sort them in various ways (for example, persons sorted as to structural principles, or roles as ethos); such orderings have in common the fact that they neglect experiencing men, usually by design. It appears that, to arrive at real behavior, the same raw facts require rearrangement. This reordering must systematically look to experiencing men.

I have described the systems of Cherokee persons and roles. In this study there is some uniqueness in that those sets of persons and roles among Cherokee men were seen as four discrete systems, four structural poses, which appeared each in its turn according to the task at hand. I now call attention to the fact that structural data, so ordered, are already in a form which makes them usable in analyzing experience based on the notion of individual. Structural pose does so in two senses.

First, data so ordered can easily be read along the axis of human life careers. In the ordering in terms of structural pose, the persons and roles expected of men in a year or a lifetime are immediately visible, each in the approximate duration and in the approximate sequence in which the society recommends that men take them up and put them down. This is the social milieu of persons and roles through which all men have lived their lives, seen in the sequence they have lived them. The lifetime person-milieu of Cherokee men is easily seen by the simultaneous inspection of Figures 2 and 4. In this sense, structural data are made available for understanding human personality.

Second, structural pose offers the data in a form which presents only those structural facts germane at the moment of acting. In this sense, structural data are made available for viewing the structural aspect of the environment in which men's acts will occur.

I have said persons and roles cannot of themselves impel men to act, hence social structure does not permit predictive understanding of behavior. Yet I have also said that these are data which (among others) are required in two crucial ways if one wishes to understand human action: ordered according to the notion of individual, the data form a social milieu through which men have moved during their lives, and a social milieu in which men stand at the moment of acting.

Structural facts ordered by the notion of structural pose admit of readings as person-facts or as individual-facts. Along the axis of person, they are read as social machinery available for work. This axis has guided this analysis up to this point. Along the axis of individual, these same facts may be read as lifetime social milieu and as social milieu at any moment. To this latter axis I now turn.

The Cherokee systems of persons and roles described cannot yet be imagined a working political system. What has been described are available social tools. We are not yet able (carefully) to imagine that these persons and roles would be taken up often, or not at all. It is necessary to imagine Cherokees coming to the moment of action with mental sets which predispose them to take up or not take up these persons and roles.

We have viewed primarily two sets of persons and roles, i.e., those for councils and for war. As person-facts the sets merely existed, available for use. As individual-facts, they enable us to see men moving into one milieu, staying for some time, then moving out and into the other. I seek now to discover whether anything can convincingly be said about Cherokee predispositions to take up or not take up those persons and roles. I seek, in other words, some support for believing that the described structures *for* politics were also the working structures *of* politics in the 18th century.

The notion of structural pose seems to fly in the face of common sense; we know well that being, say, a father tends to spill over into compartments of life where, by structural pose description, fatherhood is irrelevant. Persons do sometimes have such diffusing effects, creating predispositions to act contrary to cultural directives; however, sometimes persons do not have this effect. To understand why that does or does not happen requires analysis on the axis of the individual. We must see the variety of structural arrangements in some recurrent sequence of experience, as occasions of "input" and as occasions for "output" of psychic impulse. One virtue of the notion of structural pose is that it exactly states the problem; structural data so ordered can be read as individual-facts, as a sequence of crucial juxtapositions of structural sets as experienced by men.

Cherokee young men moved back and forth between the structural poses represented by the war organization on the one hand, and the three remaining poses on the other, hence between being structurally uncontrolled by and showing deference to old men. Deference and freedom from control entered the psychic economies of the young men, were there somehow handled, and in the handling impinged one on the other. I structure the problem with some oversimplification: I imagine that not being controlled is "easy" and that deference is "hard" and therefore imagine that the crucial psychological problem is to discover whether some predisposition to defer was somehow created in the minds of young Cherokees.

Deference to old men was recommended in the household, in the clans organized for clan revenge, and inside each clan during councils. The old men were sometimes different men (in the household as against in the clan) and different persons; to ignore these contrasts probably contains some peril. Nevertheless, I merge them, and having the data of councils in mind, I imagine this structural arrangement to stand for all. Nor, again at some peril, do I pay precise attention to the particular sequence into and out of the poses, noting only that young men moved into and out of the war organization probably four or five times during a year, for a total duration of 10 to 20 weeks.

The description in Chapter 3 of the system of persons and roles available for councils moved too easily past the crucial point now at issue. As is usual in structural studies, I then stated that the young were expected to defer to the old. If the structural pose for councils had utility to Cherokees, this expectation had to be more than an idle wish. The deference, we saw, would create a channel of influence within each clan: brother-brother relationships taken alone created no systematic channel of influence, but deference to age made of brother-brother relations tools which allowed old men to exert coercive influence over young men. Deference was a vital necessity, if village councils were successfully to arrive at a single sentiment and thereby form public policy. An apparent problem, long-standing over the Cherokee generations, was how to control again returning warriors.

We do not now attempt to span whole lifetimes. However, these young men are being viewed as moving together into and out of sets of persons and roles during a part of their lives, as having in common such a sequence of experience. We work, therefore, according to the notion of individual. (That we view these men en masse does not alter the point.) The data handled in the same way would be germane to the inquiry about kinds of Cherokee personality. I seek much less: some sense of the predispositions among all young men to defer to older clansmen.

The facts in Cherokee life, summarized under the term ethos, were, in virtual effect, an incessant pressuring for that crucial deference. We came to see ethos narrowly as an overriding lifetime moral purpose. Ethos held up circumspect conduct as the standard of moral excellence; it thereby established the criterion for honor. Ethos announced further that young men could not be expected to achieve this excellence or honor. In effect, ethos summarizes a pervading set of associations in Cherokee thought: old equals good equals honor.

Ethos, narrowly understood, was found to assert important truth about the structural poses for council and war; it is to be expected, although unexamined in these pages, that ethos would assert analogous truth about the two remaining poses. Together, the poses filled a Cherokee year. Ethos was, then, incessantly demonstrated, first one way in one pose, then another way in a second, and so on, through every Cherokee year. I rush past the details, but the implication is clear. These experiencing organisms, the young men, felt the pervading association—old equals good equals honor—in all their work and all their relations. The young men off together at war could escape bald preachment, but, as we saw, they probably acted out the same association by being "bad." In the remaining poses, that association was sometimes preached and more often demonstrated in the expressions of approval and disapproval all around.

Ethos, then, is summarized in an insistent thought: old equals good equals honor. In no visible part of Cherokee life was the thought questioned legitimately or contradicted in legitimate behavior; in no corner of Cherokee life could contrary thought or action receive support except among "partners-in-crime." This thought entails deference to age. The young men experienced that demand in what must have amounted to a virtual hammering. In such a human context, the matter must have been viewed as self-evident fact, like the sequence of the seasons. I imagine that, coming into council (or into their households or clans gathered for revenge), their disposition might often have been to yield, however difficult that might be psychologically. This does not preclude violation of the entailed directive; murders occurred in the context of such unquestionable ideas about murder. It does suggest that violations might be infrequent.[36]

The hammering of ethos possibly made the thought concerning the status of old men and the deference due them virtually unanimous. One recurrent event in Cherokee life appears to have helped young men actually to defer. The village required that warriors, on their return to the village, pass through a ritual purification. Buttrick informants (Payne MS, III:78–80) reported:

Warriors on their return from fighting continued at the council house seven days, and were cleansed by the priest for the war, nearly in the same manner, as [a family with a deceased relative]; but on some occasions they continued in their uncleanliness and separation twenty-four days, and such as had been wounded still longer, some say, seven years.

This purification can be seen as a symbolic enactment in which the freedom from restraint in the war organization was caused by ritual to pass into disuse: the young men were led to turn their minds away from war and license. This ritual purification may be viewed as a recurrent rite of passage; like all such rites of passage, this ceremony acted as a catalyst to the necessary transition by announcing: change now.[37]

Ethos is summarized in an unceasing insistence on deference; a ritual of purification pointed to the exact moment of resuming that behavior. There remains one further event in the recurrent experience of young men. Periods of required deference probably created aggressive energies but blocked their expression. Periods of relief from such demands were probably necessary, psychologically. Each war party provided such a release. However, war was largely restricted to winter, leaving six long months of the Cherokee summer, April through September, unrelieved. During these months there were the ballplays. The young men occasionally regrouped themselves, in a structure analogous to the war organization, to have inter-village ball plays, "the companion of battle."[38] Teams had [war] priests to conjure for them and after games had to pass through purifying rites analogous to the rites on return from war (Payne MS, IVb:61–64). Ballplay was a violent activity; players were as likely to maim fellow teammates as members of the other team. Also, certain roles were established for the explicit purpose of "driving" the players on to greater efforts. It is probably no accident, as a Buttrick informant reported (Payne MS, IVb:16–64), that "ancient priests [meaning the village priests who led ceremonies and councils] had nothing to do in ballplays," and that the players were ritually impure after the game.

We have stated three facts: ethos, seen as a pervading insistence on deference; ritual purification after war, seen as a rite of passage establishing an unambiguous moment to resume deferential behavior; ball play, seen as harmless release from deference (and closed also by ritual purification). These together are perhaps sufficient support for believing that young men as they entered councils might often have been predisposed to defer to age, that within each clan section the kinship persons and roles were indeed taken up often and effectively used, and that the clans were in fact working structures of Cherokee village politics.[39]

But there remains the second aspect of Cherokee councils, i.e., the work of the elders. Chapter 3 reported that the old men were expected to behave artfully toward each other with circumspection, and that it seemed that the success of this part of the council work depended on whether, in fact, they did. Hence we are not yet allowed to imagine the body of elders as a working system. The question is whether we can imagine that there was a predisposition to large effort toward the recommended moral virtuosity. That inquiry would have to proceed along the axis of experiencing individuals.

Ethos is summarized in pervading Cherokee thoughts: old equals good equals honor. Good meant artfully circumspect. These thoughts were demonstrated in each structural pose, hence unceasingly through the year. The old men had once been young men and had then experienced this insistence. Now they were old men and continued to feel it; now the lifetime goal, and the honor it entailed, were deemed within reach. There is reason to suppose that many old men might exert unusual effort toward moral virtuosity. This supposition would be strengthened by a Cherokee rite of passage to the status beloved man, but no such rite can be reported from the record.

There is cause, in sum, to imagine the Cherokee council as some kind of working system. We found reason to expect a predisposition for deference among the young men and suggested possible reasons to expect predisposition to exert unusual effort toward moral virtuosity among the old. There is cause to imagine that the persons and roles available for council were often used by young men and old, that the structure for council actually facilitated decision-making by the village, and that that political work often got done.

I suggest now a more ambitious and adequate handling of person-facts reordered as individual-facts in order to understand real behavior. I look to total life careers. In the previous section, all young men were imagined to be alike and some reason was sought in their common experience to expect a common predisposition for deference. Similarly, all old men were imagined to be alike. I now seek relatively stable individual differences in temperament or personality, that is, types of Cherokee men.

As a result of the focus in our study on the political work of adult men we have not presented data concerning the early person-milieu of Cherokee careers. It is clear that such facts might be added (if the record permits) and that they would be important for personality study; we may presume to be matters of some importance whether an infant is but one person or more, and when he begins to be different persons. Since data bearing on such points are not before us, we take, as it were, kinds of finished product, and we shall look for occasions which facilitate or hinder the expression of the psychological need of different kinds of Cherokee men. Each year's person-milieu can in our data be traced in approximate sequence for Cherokee boys. Then each year can be traced for those boys after they became young men: we know the sequence and duration of possible persons a young man could be asked to be at home, among his clan, at council, at war, and we know the role implications of those persons. Finally we can see each year of the beloved men. In short, the person-milieu of all but the earliest years of a Cherokee lifetime is available for study.

I leave aside the household and the independent clan, and consider only the council and war organization. Every young man during the year was alternately in council and on the war path, alternately vulnerable to duress from old men and free to exert his will as best he could among others free to exert theirs. There were, then, occasions for the expression of different psychic proclivities. One might easily anticipate that two individuals moving through that person-milieu might respond differently. One young man might accept the canon of deference and yield with equanimity, and another might bridle;

the first might be timid and ineffectual on the warpath, and the second might rise to great war renown. As young men became old, the milieu changed. A very few old men became war officials, and the war hero mentioned above might be a candidate for office; but for almost all old men, war activities ceased. In the body of elders, one surmises that fortunes might be reversed— the inept warrior rising to unusual influence, the war hero being awkward and ineffectual among circumspect elders.

The life careers of individual Cherokees indicate such a sorting. All men moved through the same person-milieu, and seem to have responded variously but not at random to it. We catch a glimpse, perhaps, of the variety of Cherokee personality. I briefly recount three careers and suggest others to show this variety.[40]

All three men were active during the 1750's. This decade marked the rise of tribal state. The foreign relations of the villages were at the time in great flux. Two of the men were born between 1690 and 1700, the other in the 1720's. Cherokees had traded with South Carolina since before 1710 but not substantially with any other colony. In 1753, there had been brief armed hostilities against South Carolina but the outcome had been to strengthen the alliance between the two populations. Early in 1754, however, armed conflict broke out between English and French colonies and greatly complicated the foreign relations among all tribes east of the Mississippi, and between each of the tribes and the European colonies. There were factors which pushed the Cherokees toward an alliance with the French. The western Overhills settlements were especially vulnerable to inroads by tribes allied with the French, and, by 1756, the Creeks and Choctaws from the south as well as the Shawnees from the north threatened to swing actively into the French camp. But other factors pressed the Cherokees to remain with the English. Cherokee trade with nearby South Carolina seemed more secure than any possible arrangement with the more remote French colonies on the Gulf. Further, a South Carolina garrison was building a fort in the Overhills area, and a second garrison was at an established fort in the Lower section; these garrisons offered some assurance against threats of attack but would be difficult to handle if South Carolina were hostile.

Mankiller (Outacity) of the village of Hiwasy had an uncommon career. (He was sometimes referred to as Raven; Raven was the highest war rank under Mankiller.) As suggested by his war title, he possessed the highest war honor; he was in his later years also very influential in the body of elders. In the historical record he appears as a young adult, quickly rising to prominence. At age 40 he probably led a large war party, drawn from all sections of the Cherokee area, to fight with the English against the fort at St. Augustine. Around age 50 he entered the body of elders, and was appointed the village war chief. He soon became the most influential leader among all the villages in matters pertaining to foreign relations. He wielded that influence for seven years; then, with advancing age, he relinquished his formal position but maintained a somewhat diminished influence another three years until his death. As an individual, Mankiller was extremely single-minded. In spite of the vacillating policy of Cherokee villages in their relations with the English and French, he cast his lot with the English in his youth, and he never deviated. It follows that he was not especially averse to arguing with other Cherokees. He was prone to issue peremptory orders, and to call for the punishment of individuals and even villages that seemed to him out of line. In short, Mankiller seems to have been a man destined for prominence by his effectiveness in the crisis-laden situations of warring and getting along with warriors. He was a product of competition for success in the unrestrained situation of the war organization.

In contrast with most of the warriors who became leaders in the village war organizations, he had perhaps more than usual self-control in the necessary exercise of authoritarian behavior. It is likely that he was able to exert great influence as an elder because the warriors had elected him war chief at a particularly turbulent period when defensive warfare was especially crucial. In any event, few men in Cherokee history resembled Mankiller of Hiwasy. Often, men who rose to prominence as warriors simply dropped into near-oblivion when they entered the body of elders. This, in spite of the prestige they had earned as successful warriors.

But there was another product of the war organization, more extreme than Mankiller and than those who dropped into oblivion. This man also had the title Mankiller; he was from the village of Tellico. The historical record soon shows him standing in open contempt of village and tribal opinion. The French had invited Tellico to visit their fort and establish an alliance. Though such an alliance would cut off English trade which other Cherokee villages could not allow, Tellico sent Mankiller with a party to negotiate. On his return, he worked hard to get consent for this alliance. His brother and father attempted to dissuade him; only his village agreed to join but soon even they rejected the plan. Persisting, he and a few lieutenants became effectively outcasts. Finally, Mankiller announced a change of heart; there was a brief celebration of the restored harmony in his village. Soon, however, his behavior was again reversed: he began to undertake precipitate actions in the English cause which could have induced other tribes to declare war on Cherokees, an event Tellico and the other villages were trying to prevent. Finally he came to be considered even by the English as a rogue who would do anything for a price; shortly afterwards he disappeared from the record. This product of the village war organizations found it impossible to be sufficiently responsive to public opinion to remain an accepted member of his society.

The historical record for the middle decades of the 1700's reveals the major outlines of the careers of 51 Cherokees who earned title and prestige in their youth as warriors. Of the 51, seven became markedly antisocial in the manner of Mankiller from Tellico, 25 dropped into complete or near oblivion at the end of their war careers, and 19 continued to be influential leaders, in the manner of Mankiller of Hiwasy, in the body of elders of the villages; usually they were village war chiefs.

It might be argued that there simply wasn't room at the top, as it were, in the body of elders, that all 51 successful warriors could not remain prominent as old men. But there is record of nine persons who rose to positions of great prominence in their village councils after careers as warriors which were mediocre or worse.[41] Old Hop (Canacaught) of the town of Echota (Itsati) was one of these.

Old Hop first becomes identifiable in the historical record in the 1750's as an old man in his sixties. In two years he became the most influential man of all Cherokee villages. His younger years as a warrior had been completely undistinguished; he held no war title and, on one scandalous occasion, he was held up to ridicule by an unruly young warrior because of this poor war record. Old Hop seems to have abhorred face-to-face argument. In dealing with competing French and English colonies, their allied tribes, and Cherokee villages with their conflicting interests, Old Hop consistently attempted to avoid crises—he stalled or indicated partial agreement with whichever party happened to stand before him at the moment. When Cherokees had differences among themselves, Old Hop had a great capacity to bring them together. Typically, he avoided making decisions himself. There is only one reported instance of his having ordered a Cherokee to do a thing and only two instances of his having openly opposed popular opinion. He was extremely cool-headed and patient with the more precipitate of the Cherokees around him. In short, Old Hop was a near-perfect embodiment of the Cherokee ideas about proper leadership behavior, that is, unusually circumspect. In virtue of that fact, he was able to command loyalties sufficient to override village and sectional jealousies; he was the major unifying force of his time. Six years after Old Hop appeared in the historical record, he died.

These are merest suggestions of Cherokee personalities, but students of personality and culture might find some temptation to see them sorted along a continuum of overt aggressiveness. In this light it is interesting to view the council and the war organization as two selective systems. Every living Cherokee moved through both systems. In both systems a few of these men were pushed to leadership. The appearance is that in each system a different kind of man was selected and that on a continuum of overt aggressiveness one might depict much of that difference; I make these two assumptions.

In the war organization, the more aggressive personalities moved up through the war ranks and found killing and looting congenial; this, presumably, would enhance their standing, and ranks were earned by war deeds. Our interests, however, turn more to the relations among fellow warriors. An aggressive man would be more than usually wilful and domineering over fellow warriors.

When the war organization was described, it did not seem a workable system of persons and roles, and its work appeared to be not much ordered by social structure. That was puzzling, because a war party was some kind of a social system. Men worked jointly; sometimes strategy called for large measures of discipline, for example, when an ambush was laid. It now seems possible to suggest that, if adequate facts were at hand, we might learn that Cherokee war work was performed by groups in which relations were ordered by personality. I now imagine that war relations were a kind of pecking order, a set of relations ordered by aggressive domination not unmixed with fear.

By the time some young men became old, others had died at war. In terms of personality selection, one does not know which seems more plausible: that the more aggressive, being precipitate, died; or that the less aggressive, being inept, died. (If more of the aggressive men died, the body of elders would work with less strain, but social structures do not "want" to work.) All old men were, during councils, elders. As elders we saw them operating under very demanding recommendations for conduct, patient caution being the Cherokee ethos.

It should be noted that, aside from any selection within that body, biology must have assisted in bringing these men effectively together in the person of elder. The constraint expected by them of each other, and by the village of them, was onerous. But the elders were old men, their passions had abated. Perhaps old men (when they enjoy honor and responsibility) can often attain this measure of constraint.

Within the body of elders, some old men enjoyed greater prominence than others, and the body of elders seems to have been a system for selecting leaders from the nonaggressive end of the Cherokee personality range.

In the previous section we saw reason to suppose a predisposition among elders for an unusual effort to achieve moral virtuosity. Yet, granting this, the account of the body of elders has a ring of unreality as so far described. We deal with interests, still: political systems must resolve interests and, to do so, there must be, in the nature of the case, some system of influence. Twenty or 30 old men, even trying hard to be virtuosos at decent human relations would often be at an impasse. What is lacking is a description of how some elders came to enjoy unusual influence among their fellow elders. We lack some sense of a system of influence.

The conduct recommended of elders was difficult to achieve. The presumption is that this goal was unevenly achieved, and that unequal achievement meant unequal honor. I now imagine that unequal honor meant unequal influence, and that uneven achievement thereby established uneven influence within the body of elders. Earlier, numerous social niches were found within the body of elders but no interesting details could be reported of contrasts among the corresponding roles. Too, the record was incomplete or ambiguous as to the selection of individuals to be priests or clan spokesmen. All men seem to have had access to the relevant priestly training and, if many village priests took seven pupils (one from each clan?), more individuals would be trained than could become village officials; becoming clan spokesman was not visibly determined by a ranking of lineages. The presumption is strong that clan spokesman and priest were achieved persons, and the further presumption is not unreasonable that the deciding achievement was moral virtuosity. We see then, dimly, a system of unequal influence among the elders, determined by the degree of moral virtuosity, and reflected by the persons and roles among the elders.

The suggestion is strong that those who succeeded among the elders were rarely the men who rose to higher war rank, and that these successful prominent elders were a different kind of personality and had been so through their adult lives.

All recorded careers are careers of unusual men. The average Cherokees are invisible as individuals; they must be presumed to have performed adequately but not remarkably as warrior and, later in their careers, as elder. When we look at the leaders, perhaps, we find men who are located, in terms of overt aggression, near the poles of Cherokee personality.

I notice, however, a recent report on leadership in New Guinea (Read 1959) and find there another axis of personality germane to the selection of such men. Read says:

Leadership requires a man endowed with a considerable measure of self-confidence, a person who is yielding or assertive as the occasion demands, a man who is able to judge and to wait for the appropriate moment to act, who can to a certain degree manipulate public opinion and if necessary defer to it without relinquishing either his control or his individuality, a man who is insightful and aware of group needs. Such men, I suggest, are essentially the more "autonomous" individuals in a society which Riesman would term "tradition-directed."

Read goes on to say that these respected leaders often described themselves as "bad men," and reports further:

. . . the character of leadership requires a man who has some feeling for these inconsistencies [in their culture]. It is men who possess this insight—and whose self-control enables them to profit from the knowledge—who are "selected" as leaders in the traditional sociocultural system.

These men, he notes finally, are not misfits who have no influence; they are respected leaders. Leadership in this group demands these "autonomous" qualities.

Read imagines that two inconsistent principles, "strength" and "equivalence," in Gahuku culture bring about a tension especially felt by leaders, and that this persistent tension selects or produces the kind of man who succeeds. No such inconsistency was found in Cherokee culture to make itself simultaneously felt. Yet it seems possible to find there tensions of another sort. In the war organization, there was an acultural pecking order on one side; but on the other, highest achievement lay in holding a war office, and the warriors *elected* these men. All kinds of impulsively aggressive men became Mankiller, but only some became war chief. Perhaps these elected chiefs were men with an additional measure of self-awareness and self-control. In the body of elders, still another kind of tension appears possible. On the one hand, there was the conduct necessary to maintain effective relations with elders; this required patient restraint. On the other, there was the work that a leader had to get done; this surely required some pressing at judicious moments. Again, we can suppose that among prominent elders were all kinds of unthinkingly nonaggressive men, but among the most prominent, men with an additional measure of self-awareness and self-control.

These speculations suggest that we might discover a political personality on an axis suggested by Riesman's concept of autonomy existing among all cultures but joined by other personality dimensions which vary with culture.

For our more immediate purposes I am able now to imagine the Cherokee structures for council and war as working systems. The war organization was described as unordered by social structure. It is now possible to see it raising aggressive men to prominence and thereby to see warrior relationships as a hierarchy of acultural domination, a kind of pecking order, based on personality contrasts. It is further possible to speculate that a measure of stability and judgment among warriors was provided by self-awareness and self-control among the prominent men who might often have been selected as war officials. The council enjoyed a full complement of systematic persons and roles. It is now possible to see this structure as working. We now see reasons why young men might often defer to old, and why old men might exert effort toward moral virtuosity. We also see the body of elders raising nonaggressive men to prominence and selecting prominent men with self-awareness and self-control for positions of largest influence.

Social structure is like a part of the environment even though it is carried in men's heads. Men come together bringing with them thoughts about the set of persons and roles deemed appropriate. Every man knows that every other man has the same value thoughts. This does not automatically produce action. When the Cherokee white flag went up, it was virtually automatic that people went into the council house and took appropriate seats. But the council was a web of relations making for a flow of influence. At the level where any two men confronted one another, structure was like an environment taken into account by the actors, but not automatically generative of action. A structural pose depicts such a germane environment and omits other structural facts not germane.

Besides value thoughts, each man brings to a moment of acting a kind of psychic momentum and a measure of adaptability, a personality put there in him by his unique genes and his total past experience; within that experience, one kind is unusually important, namely, his own past experiences in the set of persons he now confronts and in the other sets his society offers. The notion of structural pose offers that lifetime milieu of persons and roles in the approximate sequence in which it is lived.

With an eye to his interests and the interests of the man he confronts, with an internal momentum and adaptability and with some perception of the personality he confronts, and finally with the knowledge that both share thoughts about the persons and roles appropriate on the occasion, at least with all these, a man acts.

I recently put down the following (1958:1156):

The notion of structural pose reminds us and permits us to inquire in what way, and perhaps at what cost, the Cherokees could require any individual successfully to combine in himself the behavior required of warrior and young clansman.

The answers to that question cannot come from structural studies per se, but require help from disciplines which deal with the psychologies of individuals—role theory and depth psychology. Role theory tends to assume great flexibility in men; it anticipates and explains well the frequently large degree of success in the conscious and purposeful adjustment of a man's behavior as he moves from one role to another; the major maladjustments are expected when contradictory roles are demanded of him simultaneously. In contrast, Freudian psychology tends to insist more on the limitations of human adaptability in virtue of inborn qualities and early childhood experience; it anticipates more frequent failure, and accounts for such failures. In order to see successful flexibility or unsuccessful inflexibility, both psychologies need an image of a man's movement through the variety of social niches his society lays out for him.

Both psychologies help illuminate Cherokee social behavior. The required ritual purification of warriors on their return to the village comes to be seen as a device which insisted that the young men lay down their [unrestraint] with fellow warriors, and assume the proper [deferential] relations with their families, clans, and with villagers at large. Most young Cherokees, with the assistance of this ritual event, were successful in this recurrent adjustment. The more prominent warriors typically were not. These few remained improperly overbearing in their relations with fellow villagers, and suffered the displeasure of their fellows; they were given war honors, but otherwise avoided. Further, after prominent warriors entered the body of elders, they usually enjoyed little influence or honor. Role theory and depth psychology seem respectively best equipped to explain the usual successes and the less usual but recurrent failures. Both need structural data. Those data, in the form of structural-pose analysis, are immediately applicable to the problem; the same data, in the form of more orthodox structural analyses, are not.

I would only change it now to read that the notion of structural pose permits *students of personality and culture* to inquire into these difficult things. Structural pose does so by putting person data in a form readily usable by those who can study in terms of the notion of individual. We structuralists have the easier task.

CHAPTER 6

Comparing Political Systems

A POLITICAL system has been described which it is hoped is reasonably close to that which existed among Cherokee villages in the 18th Century. A political system includes structural poses available for work. It includes, too, men using those structures. At some one moment, a political system is one or several sets of men who are accustomed to working together with an eye to established procedures and to an audience which evaluates, and men who are able, again with an eye to procedure and an audience, to cause themselves to be systematically replaced so that the system will endure.

In this chapter, I considered two problems inherent in the comparative study of political systems. I ask, first, how political phenomena are to be consistently identified in broadly differing social orders and how, second, such phenomena once identified are to be separated into parts for comparison. The notion of structural pose seems to facilitate a useful identification of things political; this notion seems essential for finding within political phenomena parts which facilitate comparison.

Currently, there appears to be a groundswell of interest in non-Western political systems among sociologists, political scientists, and anthropologists, partly in response to the frequency with which colonies are becoming independent nations.[42] There appears also to be a fairly general sentiment that world-wide comparison—comparison among the full diversity of human political systems—is desirable and possible; generalizing science could hardly assume otherwise.

There are in the phenomenal world behaving men. Political systems are not self-evidently "out there" but are constructs by us the observers. Cross-cultural comparison of political systems presupposes that explicit criteria identify as political certain of the actions we observe. The criteria used to isolate political behavior are quite variable among students of political systems. However, there appears to be a common feature among all these sets of criteria. All students seem to agree that, when a population, acting as a single organized group, by orderly procedure binds itself to one course of action among alternative possible courses, it acts politically. It seems clear, looking over the literature on politics, that the common preoccupation is with the question: in what variety of ways do groups bind themselves to courses of action? I call this realm of political behavior "core politics."

Most students elaborate the core area, naming several aspects of this group activity, and there is much variety in the kinds of divisions made. Easton(1959) speaks of three aspects of the work of a group binding itself to a course of action:

formulating demands, legislation, administration. I have elected not to follow any of the elaborations currently employed and shall return to this point later.

Most students consider in addition to the core realm of politics other features of group life which facilitate the political work proper. Having found out the ways in which a group organizes itself politically, most students ask also such questions as the following: What is the system of recruitment for the various structural positions in which men do the core political work? In what ways does the group create adequate sentiments of solidarity and loyalty to its political structure and to the incumbents in it? In what ways does the group keep aggression under control so as to permit people to work as a political unit? These three auxiliary features—recruitment, sentiment, and control—are rightly included in a description of a political system. Most students include all three, elaborated in a variety of ways. It seems that, unless fairly arbitrary limits are established, the three auxiliary aspects together embrace virtually the totality of group life. In the descriptions of Cherokee village politics, I have touched on the three auxiliary realms of the political system but none of them was systematically and completely described. In respect to recruitment, for example, the persons among the elders were seen as partly ascribed (by age-status), partly achieved (by selection or training in moral virtuosity). But I was not able to say precisely how the movement into those positions was made. Similarly, I noted that clan revenge was an orderly procedure for checking and resolving extreme aggression within the village, and I briefly noted the apparent fact that major ceremonies created sentiments of solidarity, but these matters were cursorily handled.

In our definition of political behavior, nothing has been said so far about a monopoly of power or about coercion. "Binding" as used here must involve, in some political systems including the Cherokee, reliance on acts such as the raising of eyebrows or other mild behaviors which effect discipline. "Binding" must imply also, in some systems including the Cherokee, the option enjoyed by subgroups to remove themselves from a given course of action, so long as they do not prevent the rest from taking the chosen course. Nothing has been said, either, about a territorial estate. Almost all groups which act politically according to the above criteria do possess or control territory; but gypsies and Shoshonis do not.

A qualifying phrase appears usefully to narrow the behavior that is to be considered political: A group acts politically when it binds itself to a course of action—in matters which affect the material well-being of the population. I am now reporting thoughts which require discriminations that may prove difficult. Politics is interesting because it is the machinery through which a group, acting as a group, consciously adjusts to ongoing changes in its natural and social environment. The processes of culture change are many. Conscious group adjustment is but one process, but it has special interest because it has special practical importance. Among the judgments men and societies make, some— generally speaking, those directly affecting material well-being—have an external referent which permits that men assess the relative advantage of this or that course of action; some judgments do not have such external referent and cannot be so assessed. Corn planted two inches deep sprouts; planted 10 inches deep, it (I imagine) does not. An assessment of the risks of a raid is proved relatively accurate or inaccurate, as the case may be. With respect to securing food, warmth, physical security, etc., insofar as leadership is achieved not ascribed, men with a measure of knowledge and intelligence tend to emerge as leaders because their judgments are often proved correct. On the other hand, if a magical spell appears not to work, that tends not to cause the actors to assess the power of the spell: the logic of magic allows for counter magic. These leaders may tend to be selected "irrationally," that is, in terms of psychological needs. I am suggesting that there might be virtue in a definition which limits political action proper—the core realm of politics—to those kinds of group judgments which directly affect material well-being and therefore permit real assessment of leadership by the actors. Under contact circumstances, for example, a particular society might give the appearance of complete competence in organizing itself for ritual and yet be quite inept in adjusting to changing circumstances affecting material well-being. An indiscriminate lumping of all instances in which a group binds itself would obscure such contrasts. The two kinds of group action have, of course, very different adaptive implications. If one accepts this narrowing of the realm of core politics, one removes the bulk of materials reported as political in many British studies, for example, the materials (mainly ritual activities) in Fortes' study of Tallensi "clanship" (1945). That is not to say, however, that these same Tallensi ceremonial events might not be reintroduced as having auxiliary political functions, facilitating political action proper by creating sentiments of loyalty to the political structure and its incumbents.

A second rationale for this narrowing of the sense of political behavior may be mentioned. Redfield (1953) has distinguished two ways in which men relate to one another. Where men sort themselves and relate in terms of morally obligatory rules, the relationship is of the moral order; where men sort themselves and relate in terms of rules or agreements established by calculations of mutual expediency, the relationship is of the technical order. Relatively isolated, small societies tend to be slow-changing; under stable conditions, ways of coordinating work are not often required to change and come to be viewed through long-established practice as moral order relationships. In the world's more folk-like societies, therefore, the moral order predominates; in more urban societies, the technical order predominates; in all societies one finds a measure of both. Probably, the handling of matters materially affecting well-being— because here courses of action have obvious effects, good or ill—tend more readily to change as conditions change; new modes of coordinating work are usually of the technical order. It seemed to Redfield that, insofar as relations of a technical order exist in very folk-like societies, these tend to occur in the handling of matters of material well-being and security. In these terms and if the suggested narrowing of the meaning of core political behavior is accepted, one tends to focus on those realms where, under changing conditions, technical order relations are being by design created where moral order relations (becoming ill-adapted) once existed. Broad comparative studies of politics would then contribute, for example, to the understanding of the process of civilization, a facet of which becomes the progressive enlargement of the areas in which handlings are dictated by core political action, one aspect of the progressive encroachment of the technical order into most areas of group life. I allude here to a major *result* of political activity, the creation of new public policy (which becomes necessary when older usages no longer work). The *organization* of politics is a separate matter: a moral order system (such as the Cherokee system described here) can, of course, create technical order handlings of the matters which come before it, or that political system may change itself, becoming thereby (perhaps temporarily) a set of technical order relations.

In the above comments on the criteria by which political behavior can be consistently identified for comparative purposes, not much is new. After all it seems possible to use the focal meaning of politics generally encountered: A group acts politically when it binds itself to one course of action. Other facets of group life facilitate that activity, and these should be included in an analysis of a total political system.

I turn to the question of reducing the core realm of politics to suitable parts for comparative study. Students of sociology and persons influenced by them lean heavily on the notion of structural or functional requisites, for example, Easton. As a sort of check as to whether all the data are in a list of such requisites is essential. As a set of categories for comparative analysis, all listings seem to have a most serious difficulty: Within this crucial core area of politics —a group in the action of binding itself to a course of action—the distinctions suggested by lists of functional requisites appear impossible to make. Basically, all such lists recommend that the distinction be drawn between formulating policy and implementing or enforcing policy—a differentiation simple enough to Americans who have Congress on the one hand and the executive branch and the courts on the other.

But in the world of men without constitutions, there are only men doing things, in this instance, men making judgments affecting the actions of others. What in the abstract is the difference between making policy and implementing policy? Is one to think in terms of means and ends? Men make the judgment, say, that a war party will attack; is that forming or implementing policy? It is but a means, we might decide; the end was to wage war, and when the judgment was made to go to war, policy was formed. But it is clear also that the judgment to wage war is not self-evidently an end; the end might be to possess more horses and war would then be a means. Finally, it is clear that all group actions can be seen as means to some overriding, and never debated, end, such as the group's general welfare or, following Radcliffe-Brown, the persistence of the social structure itself. It follows that if we are abstractly to distinguish between making policy and implementing it, some line must arbitrarily and with enormous difficulty be drawn somewhere along such a means-ends chain; on one side of the line judgments form policy, on the other side, judgments are implementations. Alternatively, one might think in terms of innovation—newness against older practice. When a rule is first laid down, policy is formed; thereafter, that policy is implemented. I think it unnecessary to labor the point that whether judgments are new or old would be as difficult and as arbitrary to establish abstractly. All judgments are probably both in some admixture.

Western scientists are attracted to this distinction because Western political systems move in terms of some public awareness of it. It is an ethnographic fact, for example, that the U. S. thinks in terms of making policy as against implementing or enforcing it. A great deal of interest in the operation of American government lies in the way the country tries to live with the distinction. We argue as citizens about the legitimacy of this or that action—for example, the Supreme Court decisions on segregation—in terms of whether the action formed new policy or enforced established policy, and thus whether the action was performed by the proper governmental body. Other societies cut the pie differently and have to live with the problems raised by their categories.

We have found two organizations for categories of Cherokee core politics: councils, and war or negotiation. (I leave aside the auxiliary political task accomplished through clan revenge.) Two structures, two structural poses, handled two sets of tasks which suggests that the sets might be seen by Cherokees as two categories. Beyond that, evidence suggests that Cherokees quite explicitly saw these as discrete categories: councils (with the major ceremonies) were "white" tasks, war and negotiation (with ball play) were "red" tasks. The two categories were quite distinct, and there is evidence that Cherokees exerted some effort, for example ritual purification on return from war, to underscore the separation.

The two Cherokee categories do not coincide with Easton's functional requisites. With hindsight, the forming of corporate clan sentiments in council seems to fit nicely with Easton's formulation of demands. Similarly, the reconciliation of clan sentiments looks like legislation, and war and negotiation look like implementation. But these identifications come after the Cherokee system has been recognized, and the fit is illusory. As mentioned above, it is unclear on what abstract criteria one is able to say that a strategy judgment on the warpath, for example, a decision to call off an attack and return home, is not forming policy, i.e., legislation.

The Cherokees lived with "white" and "red" and may be presumed to have fought their political battles in those terms. A man, acting in the person of "red" war chief, was out of turn in the context of "white" council debates (unless, as when a decision for war was pending, exception was explicitly made).

The presumption is strong that, in any human society, for each category of core political action, there will exist at least one structural pose for handling that work, and that the respective structures will be importantly different according to the nature of their respective political tasks.

Comparative analysis must ask about the number and kinds of categories of political action operative in the systems we compare. Analysis in terms of the *a priori* categories suggested by listings of functional requisites would appear to obliterate those crucial facts. Besides, as I said, the distinctions appear impossible to make except arbitrarily, unless the society in question happens to make just those distinctions for us.

This suggestion is perhaps a step back from comparative analysis, toward cultural relativity in one of its manifestations. It appears, however, to be necessary. We have no sense of the types of political sortings which will be found, whether many patterns or few, because we have not asked the question. This suggestion has the additional advantage or disadvantage of being thoroughly anthropological in approach; it is very much akin, for example, to the way anthropology has gone about discovering what types of kinship systems exist.

It seems clear that the notion of structural pose makes simpler the identification of phenomena to be considered political in widely contrasting social orders. The steps were two: First, core political activities—a group acting as a unit binding itself to a course—need be identified; structural pose facilitates that identification by depicting each of the structural orderings a population can assume, some of which order that population as a single acting unit. (One then asks whether the tasks accomplished in that ordering affect material well-being or security.) Second, having identified core politics, auxiliary political activities, e.g. recruitment of personnel for the positions in core political structure(s), can be identified and analyzed.

It seems clear that the notion of structural pose is a requisite for identifying the working categories of political tasks within the general area of things political; the categories, as seen by the actors, appear essential for understanding the political system in question. The range of political work in any society seems to require a range of talents and procedures. The presumption is strong that the contrasting talent and procedures will segregate as separate structural orderings, and that these discrete structural poses will mark, in the minds of the actors, the categories of political work in terms of which their system runs.

PART II

BEYOND THE FACE-TO-FACE COMMUNITY

We are now Building a Strong
House, and the very first of our
People, that does any dammage
to the English, shall be put in
there. . . . (Williams 1937:267–68)

CHAPTER 7

Peace Among Independent Equals: To 1730

THE Cherokee tribe before 1730 was a jural community; Cherokee villages, although they recognized no higher authority, did not often war on one another. Among them, there was a sentiment of obligation to settle disputes peaceably, and there were persons and roles which helped make that possible.[43]

This chapter looks outside the independent sovereign villages and describes their relations one with the other. I then make brief mention of the persons and roles which were available to maintain peaceful coexistence among the villages before 1730.

The Cherokees experienced little direct contact with Europeans before 1699. In 1540 De Soto traveled through the Southeast; whether or not he encountered the Cherokees is still debated. In 1577, the Spaniard Juan Pardo established forts in the area of present-day South Carolina, but his contact, for the short duration of those posts, was with the Creek. Jamestown was established in 1607. By the 1650's and 60's, Virginia traders were active in the Appalachian mountainous areas to the west, but according to all clear reports their trading was with Siouan-speaking tribes. In the 1670's, Charles Town was established, and the initiative in westward expansion passed to Carolina. From the outset, Carolinians dealt largely with the Cherokees. By 1693, the relations between the Cherokees and Carolina had developed to the point that a Cherokee group went to Charles Town to complain about slave raids (Salley 1907:12). And by 1694, Carolina traders were probably established on rivers which emptied westward into the Mississippi (Williams 1937:26).

But in 1699, the French occupied Lousiana, and the struggle between France and England over the southeast began. From that point forward, with only intermittent interruptions, the Cherokee villages and Carolina were allied against France and French tribes; the Cherokees became increasingly important to Carolina, and Carolina to the Cherokees.

By 1707, Carolina trade relations with the Cherokees had increased enough to cause the Charles Town government to enact its first trading act (Williams 1937:63–64). That first act was inconsequential and short-lived; in 1712, the government passed a second act (Jenkins 1949:June 7, 1712). In 1715, relations became hostile for a brief period when many Cherokee villages joined the Yamassee War against Carolina. A Carolina detachment was sent to the Cherokees to dissuade them, and the hostile villages readily withdrew from the war (Willis 1955:44–45). Then, in 1716, a third and much more thorough trading act was enacted (Jenkins 1949:April 30, 1716). The new act established governmental trading posts in several of the larger Cherokee villages.

Cherokee relations with Europeans had steadily increased but, up to 1730, these relations probably were less frequent and less crucial than the accustomed relations between the Cherokee villages and Indians of other tribes. Warfare with Europeans was less frequent and probably only slightly more destructive, so arms were not yet a matter of life and death; nor were there other cultivated needs which made trade with Europeans indispensable.

Cherokees were surrounded by tribes with whom there were frequent hostilities; at other times relations of trade and more casual contacts existed. To the south were the Muskogean-speaking tribes (and others) of the Creek confederacy; with these, there was much contact, often hostile. To the southwest were the Chickasaw and Choctaw. To the northeast were the Shawnee, strongly in the French alliance and hostile almost without interruption. To the northeast were small Iroquoian-speaking tribes and, beyond them, the Iroquois League itself with whom there were frequent wars. Immediately to the east there were for a few years small seaboard tribes, Yuchi, Yamassee, and others; but they soon moved or disappeared, leaving the Colony of South Carolina the immediate neighbor.

Cherokee relations with Europeans and Indians were under the jurisdiction of each of their independent villages. A decision by a village as to a course of action was, however, subject to outside influence and, from the first, sporadic coordination of actions by several villages occurred. Cherokee villages shared an identical culture; all spoke one of three mutually intelligible dialects; members of one village shared a dialect with some 15 other villages. All Cherokees shared a common history, although the villages of the Lower Cherokees probably came to their location on the headwaters of the Savannah via a route east of the Appalachian Mountains, while the Middle, Overhill, and Valley sections of the Cherokees came directly from the west. This separation was probably of short duration, and the two divergent histories were mutually understood and in this sense shared. Common culture, language, and history no doubt led young warriors, acting as individuals, to join voluntarily war or hunting parties from other villages.

A few villages were able to exert especially great influence. To different European observers, some half dozen villages appeared at different times to be the tribal "capital," and their officials the tribe governors.

The Cherokee tradition spoke of seven mother villages which wielded great influence in ceremonial affairs. Probably, these villages were intellectual centers, where priests, as primitive intelligentsia, worked toward systematization of the traditional beliefs. An informant told Buttrick (Payne MS, IVa: 159–60):

The Cherokees, as far back as their history can be traced, have been divided into at least two sects. That which embraced the great body of the people and gave a stamp to their rational character, was evidently idolatrous . . . . The other sect embracing but few, comparatively, say that there existed Three Beings above, always together, and of the same mind. . . . The difference between this sect and the former seems to have consisted only in the objects of worship, and not in outward form and ceremonies.

The priests in those centers probably exerted great influence in religious matters on other priests throughout the tribe. Because the ceremonial leaders in Cherokee villages were also the great influences in village general councils, it is probable that the priests in these mother villages wielded much influence throughout the tribe in political matters as well.

But the historical record is inconsistent as to which villages were the mother villages. Probably, the actual influence of a village tended, over time, to make it a mother village. There was some overt competition among villages for influence, as in matters of trade. But the influence of any village was largely determined by its location. It could be dangerously exposed to an enemy or protected; it could be accessible to a trading power or less accessible. As alliances came and went, and as hostilities flared and died out, village fortunes rose and fell. In these early years, Lower villages were predominant over other sections because they were closest to South Carolina. The early prominence of Tugalo and Keowee, for example, was probably the result of their being the first villages encountered by travellers moving upstream along each of the two main branches of the Savannah River. On the other hand, the Overhills villages were most easily reached from Virginia, but Virginia at this time did almost no trading. For reasons impossible to discern in the record, however, the influence of Overhills villages was relatively strong. As early as 1715, the Overhills section was termed (Williams 1937:72–73) the most "vigorous" part of the tribe.

For one short period of four or five years, Cherokee relations with South Carolina were largely in the hands of one man. An unnamed priest of a Lower village, Tugalo, became the most influential man of the tribe, in the eyes at least of Carolina officials. He was first mentioned (Willis 1955:210) in 1715, when army officers went to the Tugalo council house to negotiate with the tribe; there "ye Congyrer satt in State to Recive" them. For the next four or five years there were repeated negotiations in matters of trade. "Chiratahigi" as he was usually called (meaning high priest [Adair 1775:80]) was the central figure in all these meetings.

Chiratahigi enjoyed unusual but informal influence, and, by and large, Carolina recognized the absence of a tribal governmental structure. When large matters were to be decided, the Charles Town government usually invited, as in 1821, "a Head man out of each Town" (Salley 1930:18). Even during the peak of Chiratahigi's influence, a meeting in Charles Town was referred to as a conference with the "Charikee Kings and other great Men of that Nation" (Jenkins 1949:Jan. 29, 1717). South Carolina officials had first hand knowledge that his powers were limited. In a conference, beginning April 30, 1716, Chiratahigi was induced to promise that young Cherokees would transport South Carolina's trade goods from Savannah, and Cherokee furs to Savannah. Probably much maneuvering among the villages followed: In order to produce the carriers he promised, Chiratahigi was forced to go repeatedly to the South Carolina officials and ask for modifications of the plan. But the Overhills villages refused. Finally, traders had to be established in the larger villages throughout the tribe to permit men from each vicinity to carry on their own trade exclusively (Jenkins 1947: July 10, 1716 to June 14, 1718).

In 1719 or 1720, Chiratahigi died. No one was able to step into the place of influence of the Tugalo priest. In the following months, different observers reported the predominance of Mankiller of Toxawa, a Lower village; others reported the predominance of Kenotiski of an unnamed village; by 1725, South Carolina acted as if there were four prominent men, two from the combined Overhills, Valley, and Middle sections, and two from the Lower section (Salley 1945:29).

There are no records of actual warfare between Cherokee villages. Mooney (1900:377) reported a myth which alluded to threatened hostility; perhaps they occurred on rare occasion.

In sum, villages varied in size and influence; they coexisted peacefully, and on intermittent occasions there was coordination among villages. Peaceful coexistence and intermittent cooperation were managed without a specific organization for tribal politics; there were no tribal officers and no tribal procedures for decisions by the tribe at large.

Among Cherokees, there was a restraining sentiment that villages should peacefully coexist. That sentiment appears to have stemmed from a common history. In the human world, however, sentiments of restraint seem not sufficient unto themselves and, left alone, seem soon to dissipate; such sentiments usually require that they be borne by institutionalized social machinery; these can channel men's public behavior, and thereby assist in keeping the sentiments alive by the very practice of them.

The persons and roles which could keep such Cherokee sentiments alive and permit their expression were of two sorts: Cherokee men had fellow clansmen in every village, and virtually every Cherokee man had fathers, brothers, and other blood relatives in some village other than his own.

Every village contained members of each of the seven Cherokee clans. The seven clan sections inside each village were on occasion corporate groups. The seven clans, tribe-wide, were not on any occasion acting groups. They were, however, seven statuses, and as statuses had important uses. A man of the wolf clan found in any village members of the wolf clan. Upon his arrival in a village, he identified himself as to clan and by this identification could assume a fictive place in the village. He was brother to members of the wolf clan section of the village, and they were brother to him; other members of the village were of course in some relationship (depending on pose) to members of the wolf clan section, so they could readily devise ways to relate to him, by extension, as the brother of this or that wolf clansmen.

As suggested in Chapter 1, the Cherokee rules of incest, plus mere facts of demography, assured that many Cherokee men would marry into other villages. Fathers, mothers, and other relatives would usually remain in the home village and be potential channels of influence over the affairs of the home village. It follows that those relatives in turn would have the reverse entree into his village.

Further, several brothers might marry into several villages, extending a web of kin ties.

It is possible to see these intervillage ties as potential tools for effecting co-ordination among villages at war with a tribe or with colonial power. It is also possible and probably more important to see how the ties of clan might be crucial in instances of personal killing or injury of individuals from different villages. The institution of clan revenge made of such an event a clan matter. A killing was an affair, essentially, between the clan section of the killer, in one village, and the clan section of the killed, in another; but both sections had clan brothers in the opposite village. The presumption is that the obligations among clan brothers, if invoked, would be a virtual guarantee that the affair not become village versus village, but be resolved between the involved clan sections. That these ties actually worked as suggested is presumptive. The record does not say.

This brief chapter has sketched the outlines of organization of a jural community. The notion of a jural community is important because it calls attention to and provides a name for a state of relationships recurrent in human affairs. Independent political communities, recognizing no other authority, often share a long-standing sentiment that differences between them ought to be settled peaceably and employ mutually acknowledged traditional procedures which facilitate the resolution of differences. Among more complex societies where politics is formalized by written codes and constitutions, we find the word alliance applied to a peaceful state of affairs between sovereign states. This is not quite the sense in which we here employ jural community, because some alliances may come and go and are sometimes seen as momentary conveniences, while others are more permanent. The "English-speaking nations" are a jural community; perhaps the world of major powers is becoming one.

Before 1730, the Cherokee tribe was a jural community. It was an aggregate of politically independent, that is, sovereign villages in permanent peaceful coexistence. The sentiment for settling disputes peaceably was probably made workable and kept alive by fictive tribewide clan brotherhood, and by an un-systematic web of blood kinship across the villages.

There are three levels of political organization which appear to be human universals:

1. *Sovereignty.* It seems useful and possible to locate in any human aggregate the widest body which acts as a political unit, that is, the most inclusive body which acts to bind itself to a course of action in matters affecting material welfare. These are sovereignties. A Cherokee village was a sovereignty until 1730, as is the United States.

2. *Jural community.* One locates the boundaries of a jural community in any human aggregate by discovering where, in the relations among sovereign-ties, action is limited and follows some common established procedures. Rela-tions between sovereignties within a jural community are mutually restricted.

Such relations seem advantageous to the sovereignties involved in terms of long-term expediency. The Cherokee tribe was a jural community until 1730, as are the English-speaking nations.[44]

3. *The political environs.* This category is residual. It labels those people who, from the point of view of one society, are outside their jural community but with whom there are recurrent (but usually infrequent) contacts. The relations are unrestricted; a sovereignty acts toward such other sovereignties in terms of calculations of immediate expediency.

Beginning in 1730, the Cherokees slowly transformed their jural community and made of it a state; the sovereign villages were gradually, through some trial and error, to give up their independence and create a single tribal sovereignty, the Cherokee priest-state.

CHAPTER 8

Toward a Tribal State: 1730-1761

I DESCRIBE now the slow creation by Cherokees of a system of persons and roles to do the political work for the tribe as a whole. It became apparent by 1730 and thereafter that the Cherokees were to share a common fortune. Tangible events were to underscore that new social fact in the experience of every Cherokee. South Carolina had decided to act in some crucial matters as if the tribe were a political entity. Henceforth, the action of one Cherokee could bring reprisal against any Cherokee. The reprisal-provoking Cherokee actions could be raiding the colonial frontier, or molesting colonial traders. South Carolina could send troops, or cut off trade; both, from this point forward, could be exceedingly hurtful. The essential political problem facing the tribe was to create a method for the prevention of unauthorized violence by their warriors. It required more than 30 years to achieve a more or less adequate solution.

I describe first the development, starting in 1730, of gross social machinery for handling relations with South Carolina, constituted by a quasi-government of warriors, and modeled after one of the village political structures, the war organization. I then narrate the history of development through the 1750's of the Cherokee priest-state, a replica of the two village structures for politics, the council and the war organization. Finally, I ask in what measure the priest-state structure of persons and roles was adequate to the political tasks it faced. Village political systems continued without modification during this period of the creation of a tribal state. The villages gave up their sovereignty when the tribe took over foreign affairs, but continued to fulfill other functions.

The first tribal structure for political work was analogous to the village structure for offensive war; its function was to become, like that of the same village structure, negotiation with foreign powers, mainly with South Carolina, on matters of trade. The action of a single Cherokee could bring reprisals against all Cherokees. The tribal officials could, through negotiations and coercive punishments of Cherokees, stop the reprisals. Such actions were a first step toward tribal government, but they could not prevent unauthorized raids.

In 1730, the gross beginnings of an explicit structure for tribal political work were created through the action of some of the villages and at the suggestion of an eccentric Scotsman. That year, Sir Alexander Cuming marched through the Cherokee country. By the time he had completed his calls on most of the larger villages, these villages, at his prodding, had chosen as "Emperor" of the tribe, one Moytoy of the Overhills village Tellico, probably the war chief of that village (Drake 1872:13). This action, however, seems not to have been accepted by many villages; 20 years were to pass before this tribal institution appeared well established.

In the early 1730's, Georgia was founded, and North Carolina split off from the Charles Town government. Both new colonies soon became competitive in the Indian trade; Virginia traders were already stirring. In 1734, a handful of Cherokees seized the goods of a South Carolina trader. South Carolina demanded payment, was refused, and retaliated by cutting off the Cherokee trade. Virginia attempted to send in trade goods but was forcibly stopped by South Carolina; the Cherokees sent a delegation to Charles Town. South Carolina used the incident to strengthen her position by purchasing from the Cherokees land in the Lower section for a fortified trading post (Grant 1909:58). This purchase was negotiated with some 70 Cherokee leaders, all from villages in the Lower section; apparently, there were no negotiations with Moytoy (Weber 1918:157–61).

In 1738–39 smallpox struck the tribe, killing perhaps half the population. The "doctors"—probably war surgeons—were unsuccessful in their attempts to cure. Individually, they appear to have lost much prestige, and they destroyed their ritual paraphernalia (Adair 1775:232). This epidemic seems not to have affected the Moytoy government. In 1739, the tribe had a poor harvest. Georgia sent 1,500 bushels of corn to help avert famine (Candler 1904–16, V:239).

In 1741, Moytoy died; he was succeeded by his son, Amouskositte of the same Overhills village, Tellico (Willis 1955:94). There was some resistance to the succession, probably from the Lower villages. A Georgia army officer reported of a meeting of "the Head Men of all the Cherokees" (he stated erroneously) who selected for "Emperor" the war chief of the Lower village Keowee (Candler 1904–16, XVII:195–96). But the influence of the Overhills villages, always great for unknown reasons, was becoming greater for two reasons clearly stated in the record. First, there had been marked decline in Chickasaw military strength which left the Overhills villages facing the French and tribes allied to the French. Thus those villages became of military importance to all the English colonies to the east. Second, Virginia had fully entered the Indian trade, and Virginia traders went naturally to the easily accessible Overhills area. Probably because the Overhills section was increasingly influential, Amouskositte of Tellico was able to overcome opposition from other sections.

For four years, beginning in 1744, France and the English colonies were at war. By and large, the Cherokees remained allied with the English. But tribes allied with the French periodically caused serious casualties, especially in the Overhills area; villages responded by periodically making overtures for peace to the French side. One rising Cherokee star from the Overhills section, The Little Carpenter, was in the enemy camp as a negotiator throughout the war. It is unclear to what degree these conflicting tendencies of Cherokees were coordinated strategy decided in Tellico or the uncoordinated actions of villages acting independently. The presumption is strong that the strategy was uncoordinated; war organizations had traditionally implemented, not formed, policy.

In 1746 a prominent Cherokee warrior killed a South Carolina trader. Again, trade was cut off and the Governor of South Carolina demanded that the killer be turned over; the killer's village refused. The loss was serious because of the vulnerability of Cherokees to raids by French-allied tribes. A meeting was called, presumably by Amouskositte, which "resolved to reduce the town to ashes and massacre its people, if they did not yield up the murderer, or put him to death themselves. They consented [and shot him]" (Logan 1859: 456–57).

At the close of the French-English war, intense hostilities began between Cherokees and Creeks. Creek attacks on the Lower villages were so severe that all but two or three villages were abandoned. South Carolina and South Carolina traders attempted to maintain peaceful relations with both sides. Since the most important trade items were guns and ammunition, the South Carolina policy was unworkable. In early 1751, two traders with a Creek war party were killed by Cherokees; South Carolina attempted to have the killers punished. A group of young Cherokees retaliated by raiding the trading post in their village. Rumors of armed reprisal by South Carolina swept the Cherokees villages, and other trading posts were raided. Georgia and South Carolina cut off the trade. Scattered Cherokee war parties marched against colonial frontier settlers (Jenkins 1949: February–May, 1751).

Amouskositte and the war leaders around him attempted to quiet the tribe, calling a meeting on May 1, 1751. Amouskositte, rather pathetically, sent word to the Governor of South Carolina that he did not know what to do, that he could not sleep nights, and so on (Jenkins 1949: May 1, 1751). However, by September he apparently felt more sure of his ground; he wrote and asked for trade, promising that, if a trader should be hurt, the guilty Cherokee would die (Jenkins 1949: September 22, 1751). Finally, in November, he assembled 17 prominent men, at least 11 of whom were distinguished war leaders, from 13 large villages. This party traveled to Charles Town and negotiated a peace treaty which provided that certain guilty Cherokees would be turned over to South Carolina, and that the traders would be reimbursed for the goods taken from them; South Carolina agreed to certain new trading regulations the Cherokees requested (Jenkins 1949: November 14–28, 1751). The treaty provided for reestablishing trade with Charles Town. It was the last significant act of Amouskositte's government.

This government of warriors had been created at the urging of an eccentric Scot, but had persisted. During Moytoy's years, the "Emperor" came to be seen, by some of the tribe, as a person—a structural niche which could be considered as being empty and, if empty, calling for an occupant. Nothing is known of structural details; probably the structure was amorphous, as were the village war organizations on which it was modeled.

This structure for political work persisted because there were tasks to be fulfilled—new tasks demanded by a new Cherokee situation. Three times, in

1734, 1746, and 1751, a similar sequence of events had occurred. One Cherokee, or a few, had harmed a trader; then trade had been cut off. In two of the instances, the loss of the ammunition supply was especially damaging because of war with neighboring tribes. For the first time in Cherokee history, it became a recurrent fact that members of all villages suffered by the action of some one member of some one village. In short, South Carolina behaved as if all villages together were a political entity sharing group responsibility for the actions by any of its members. It must be presumed that Cherokees had become aware that unauthorized raids had to be prevented, not only punished. During the years since 1730, the group responsibility ascribed by South Carolina to the tribe at large had become evident to many, perhaps all, Cherokees; and, during these years, the life and death importance of trade had become equally evident.

In effect, the tribe here faced a choice. It could become a tyranny and thereby prevent misdeeds. One thoughtful Cherokee supposed it could. In 1752, an outstanding warrior wrote the Governor: There are rogues among us, he said, but my people "will break them" because we must have ammunition (Jenkins 1949: March 31, 1752). He was assuming a climate of fear. But the traditional value attached to circumspect behavior entailed a traditional abhorrence of physical coercion, and the long-standing ambivalence toward warriors virtually assured that Amouskositte and his lieutenants would exercise coercion gingerly or become ostracized.

Tribal instincts or habits, or genius, or all three, caused men to choose, slowly through trial and error, quite another course: the creation of a priest-state. The governments of Moytoy and Amouskositte had been a development from the village war organizations. Moytoy probably had been war chief of Tellico just prior to being named Emperor. Amouskositte's career, before he became Emperor, is unknown; but the men he gathered around him were largely, probably exclusively, prominent warriors (Jenkins 1949: November 14–28, 1751). The job those governments attempted was a single, limited task theretofore done by village war organizations; they negotiated with foreign powers.

In a Cherokee village, however, the war organization was but a part of the social structure for political work. Through these 20 years of tribal politics, there was no discernible tribal structure analogous to the village structure for village councils. In the villages, a party of negotiators ideally left for foreign parts with directions from the village councils; if the delegation decided in the negotiations to make commitments, there was the village council to receive its report, to discuss it, to form a public sentiment which accepted it or rejected it. These early tribal governments had no equivalent way to articulate themselves to the populace.

In spite of his apparently adequate handling of the crisis of 1751, the "Emperor" rapidly lost influence in the months which followed. By July 1753, Old Hop of the Overhills village Echota emerged as the *de facto* leader of the tribe (Logan 1859: 461–63). Amouskositte continued to be referred to as "Emperor" but within three years South Carolina officials recognized that he was without influence except in his own village, that the great center of Cherokee influence had become Echota (Willis 1955:255), and that the greatest influence in Echota was Old Hop. He was, unlike Amouskositte, a beloved man, the speaker (the highest secular official among the elders) in his village (Jenkins 1949:April 22, 1752). A new step toward the prevention of unauthorized raids was in process.

In 1753, the old beloved men entered politics on the tribal level. Under the leadership of Old Hop of Echota, they pushed Amouskositte aside and, for some five years, operated without a formal governmental structure. By 1758, the structure of this first tribal state had become explicit. The first Cherokee state included, as the Amouskositte government before it, a tribal structure for implementing policy, modeled after the village structure for war. It also included a structure to form policy very similar to the village structures for councils—a means by which the tribe at large could form and express a single public sentiment.

Old Hop and the beloved men around him led tribal affairs for five years without an explicit structure. Cherokee relations with foreign powers during those five years were enormously complex. England and France were again moving toward war as armed clashes between their colonials became increasingly frequent. Inevitably, the tribes were drawn in. The French-allied tribes to the north and west raided more often the exposed Cherokee villages. In the south, Cherokees were at war with the Creeks; and from the east, English settlers were making the first serious inroads on Cherokee land (Jenkins 1949: February 11, 1756). The Old Hop government aimed to preserve the flow of trade from the English colonies, especially guns, and to induce these colonies to build and man forts in the most exposed Cherokee areas. At the same time Old Hop did not wish to provoke French tribes to still stronger attacks on vulnerable Cherokee villages. This policy was difficult to carry out when encroaching English settlers from time to time provoked Cherokee villages to retaliatory raids on the English frontier.

The Cherokee priest state emerged during those complex years. The first distinct sign was recorded in 1753, when the Governor of South Carolina asked for a Cherokee delegation to come to Charles Town; the Little Carpenter was sent and announced that he spoke for Old Hop, "the great beloved wise man of the Nation" (Logan 1859:460). A new political person was in the making; Old Hop never became "Emperor."

From the outset, there was some opposition to Old Hop's leadership. As late as June, 1756, spokesmen for villages in the Lower section sent word to the Governor that, although he had sent a message to the Overhills, any message he might have for the Lower villages "must be directed to the Chiefs of the five Lower towns." They further asked the Governor to divide any presents sent to the tribe in order to "prevent any differences arising betwixt them and the Overhills." They claimed to speak also for the Middle villages (Jenkins 1949: June 23, 1756). When in July 1756, the "Emperor" Amouskositte made a new bid for supreme power by forming and leading a delegation to Charles Town, the Little Carpenter, Old Hop's delegate, met the party en route and a South Carolina official reported "a great Coolness . . . betwixt the two parties" (Jenkins 1949: July 13, 1756).

Coordination of tribal affairs around Old Hop was, however, taking place. In the fall of 1756, Old Hop sent word to the Middle and Lower villages that he could be found at Echota all winter. When the young men of the Overhills area went out for their winter hunt that year, a system of communication was set up with Old Hop which could have many of them back in the village in two or three days (Jenkins 1949: November 13, 1756). In December of 1757, Old Hop was able to soothe the feelings in a distant village of the family of a man killed by an English trader and thus prevent reprisals (Jenkins 1949: December 12, 1757).

By April 1758, the Middle village Jore, in response to a request of South Carolina, refused to answer until they consulted Echota "as it is the beloved Town that all the other Towns in the Nation Regards" (Jenkins 1949: April 13, 1758). Probably by this date, the priest-state under Old Hop had become an accomplished fact, a tribal government with at least the outlines of formal organization and procedure.

It is germane to relate a series of events during these formative years demonstrating the degree of independence still enjoyed by the villages. The events also show exercise of influence among members of separate villages, largely through kin ties; this intense scurrying about seems to have stemmed from widespread recognition that the tribe shared a common fate and from the palpable threats to that general interest. The events dimly show, finally, the hand and influence of Old Hop. The central actor was Mankiller of Tellico.[45]

In 1756, in the midst of the struggle between France and England and the complex involvement of Cherokees in that struggle, Mankiller made overtures to the French. He received a reply inviting a parley. On September 28, Mankiller and his negotiating party left for a French fort in Alabama, apparently with the full approval of his village.

Throughout the villages, no vocal opposition to Mankiller's trip to the Alabama fort is recorded, probably because the trip might forestall attacks by French Indians. But probably there was also little sentiment, except in Tellico, for the unequivocal French alliance Mankiller and the French had in mind.

On November 8th, messengers were sent back from Mankiller's party. They reported to Tellico glowingly of French gifts of arms, ammunition, and other goods, and they told how French officials had taken some of the party on to New Orleans to meet the French Governor. Most importantly, they told of a plan that had been devised: if Tellico would move west and establish a new village on the Hiwasee River, the French would send a great supply of arms as a present, would establish a fort there for Tellico's protection, and would assure them abundant trade in the future. The Tellico population moved out of their village and set to work building new homes at the chosen site. The village of Chatuga, which was immediately next to Tellico and usually intimately associated, refused to go.

By November 25th, a handful of Tellico elders returned from the new village and proclaimed their loyalty to the English. On December 8th, Mankiller traveled to the

Overhills village, Echota, the home of Old Hop, and there met for two days with many of the outstanding men of several Overhills villages. After the meeting, these men informed South Carolina officials that Tellico was "but one town," disassociating their villages from Tellico's actions.

Mankiller's brother, Kenetote, who lived in Old Hop's village, went to the English fort and talked long with the commander, Captain Demere. Then he went to see Mankiller and later told Demere he had caused Mankiller to "cry bitterly" by reproaching him for his deeds. But houses were still going up at the site of the new village. At the same time, Demere distributed presents to Overhills villages, ostentatiously giving none to Tellico.

By January 2, 1757, Demere reported that he felt Mankiller was "on the spot" because all the villages had so clearly divorced themselves from the action of Tellico. Apparently, sentiment inside Tellico had begun to shift. An attempt was made to get Mankiller to talk with an old trader at the home of Mankiller's father at the Overhills village, Settico, but Mankiller was "ashamed" and would not come.

On January 5th, Mankiller came to Demere at the fort, in a very "cross" mood. They had a long confessional-like conversation in which Mankiller complained that everyone had put all the blame on him, that he was hated by all the Cherokee, that he hadn't known what to do, but that, now that Demere had given him such a good talk, he knew. Then Mankiller's young men arrived, 150 strong, and all were given a feast. Mankiller slept at the fort that night and the next day he took under his protection two English traders who had earlier fled from Tellico and returned with them to the original Tellico village which was apparently being reoccupied.

By January 11th, all the people had returned and, on that day, a great feast and dance was given at Tellico. Lieutenant Robert Wall, one of Demere's junior officers, went to Tellico, was received with great courtesy and feasted. Over two hundred adults gathered at the council house. Mankiller ceremoniously shook hand with Wall, then everyone filed past to take Wall's hand. Lieutenant Wall gave a talk and remarked later that there was "nothing but the greatest order, Decorum, & Attention. . . . the Headmen giving the usual word of Assent and approbation to every Sentence." Then Mankiller spoke of how the thoughts of Tellico had been bad, how their breath had been infected, but they now knew that Demere was a friend and brother and all were children of King George. That evening Tellico gathered again at the council house. Lieutenant Wall was again received with great joy. Mankiller said that he never danced except on extraordinary occasions but that tonight he would because his heart was light. He returned with fifty-seven warriors, all painted. The assembly let out a shout, the drums began, and for one hour the warriors danced around the fire, then the older men joined for three more hours, then the men stopped and the young women danced, and finally the older women joined them. At 2:00 A.M., Lieutenant Wall indicated he would go to bed. Mankiller caused the music to stop and a prominent villager spoke at great length, how their thoughts had been bad but were no longer, and how they would send this word to Echota and the other villages.

In the next day or two, Demere saw Old Hop and remarked that the old man was "very merry." Old Hop had called a meeting of all the Overhills villages for January 16 at Echota to take Demere "by the hand" and swear their friendship to the English. At that meeting, Old Hop and Demere publicly embraced one another "to the joy of" the assembled Cherokee.

When Demere returned to the fort, Mankiller was there, this time supported by his brother. Both discussed the difficult position of Tellico in regard to trade and aired certain grievances about past actions by traders which had helped bring on the trouble.

On March 14th, Mankiller called at the fort to ask for arms to go against the French Indians. Apparently, much in Mankiller's behavior remained suspect but Demere decided to trust him because of the great pressures which still were on Mankiller from his villagers and other Cherokee—"they Plague him to Turn good."

On March 20th, the Tellico party which had gone to New Orleans returned. Mankiller appeared before his father's house at Settico with nothing on but a ragged blanket, to indicate how poor they were without French trade; he was sent away by the old man. Demere remarked that Mankiller was now discredited within his village and throughout the tribe, except for a few close associates.

In spite of Mankiller's display of apparent reconciliation with the sentiments of his own villagers and of the Cherokees at large, apparently, the pressures had not brought adequate results.

On July 30th, Mankiller reappeared at the fort with an old scalp, claiming he had killed a French Indian and asking the reward which was refused. Demere reported that now everyone was against Mankiller, even his brother Kenetote. But Demere recognized in Mankiller a new utility, as a "rogue" who would do anything for presents, and offered him a reward for killing a Frenchman and a Shawnee in the vicinity, long-time residents among the Cherokee and reliable messengers from the Cherokee to those groups, whom the Cherokee had repeatedly refused to turn over to the English. Mankiller accepted.

Mankiller then drops from the historical record.

In September of 1758, an event tipped the balance of Cherokee foreign affairs and seven months later brought on war with the English. A Cherokee party had joined the successful English attack on the French at Fort Duquesne. The returning party had a skirmish with Virginia settlers; several warriors were killed. Some villages immediately sent parties against the Virginia frontier. Old Hop waited three months until the party returned, meanwhile holding consultations with the old leaders of Echota. The party returned and pressed for war with the English (Williams 1937:210–24). Old Hop had become very old and sick. On May 2, 1759, Old Hop appeared in the record for the last time. On or about May 3, one village had sent a large party against the frontier killing frontiersmen (Jenkins 1949: May 3, 1759); soon other parties from other villages followed. In September Quebec fell to the English. In October, a delegation led by the tribal war chief, Great Warrior (Aganstata), left for Charles Town. When they reached Fort Prince George in the Lower section, they were imprisoned by South Carolina and held as hostages to force the Cherokees to turn over to Charles Town a number of Cherokee warriors equal to the number of Englishmen killed on the frontier. Little Carpenter went to Charles Town and managed to get Great Warrior and three or four of the others released. During the winter, many of the hostages died of smallpox in prison. In February 1760, through a ruse by a band of Cherokee warriors, the English commander of the fort was enticed outside the fort and mortally wounded. The soldiers killed the remaining hostages; war broke out (Jenkins 1949: February 8–17, 1760). In June, English armies destroyed the Lower and Middle villages and returned to South Carolina (Schoolcraft 1860, III: 240). In August, Cherokees under Great Warrior obtained the surrender of Fort Loudon, the newly constructed South Carolina fort in the Overhills, and then killed the garrison (Saunders 1886–90, VI:313–15). In June of 1761, the Middle villages were again burned by English armies. Great Warrior made overtures for peace, and on August 28, Little Carpenter and 30 other Cherokees negotiated a peace treaty. On this occasion, Little Carpenter announced, "Our Head man, Old Hop, is gone to sleep, and the Standing Turkey has come in his room . . . " (Williams 1937:269).

Standing Turkey had first appeared in the record only a few years earlier; then he was already an old man. He was a close associate of Old Hop's, probably the priestly village messenger of Echota (Jenkins 1949:November 13, 1756). During these two and one-half years of war, only the names of prominent warriors appear in the record. But the appointment of Standing Turkey in Old Hop's position as "great beloved wiseman of the Nation" is evidence that the structure for tribal politics had not been basically altered.

The informants of Buttrick have left us the materials for a reasonably full description of the system of persons and roles made available for tribal politics.[46] This priest-state was modeled after Cherokee village organizations for general council and offensive war. The Cherokee tribe now had a structure like every Cherokee village for handling the full range of political tasks. There was an explicit organization for decision-making (and for festivals) on a tribal level and there was a less well-defined tribal organization for implementing the more crucial decisions through war and foreign negotiations.

When the whole tribe convened for councils, the white standard of the capital village was raised. At least once a year, and certainly on the occasion of the capital village's New Year's council, a tribal council took place.[47] At the apex of the tribal government was the body of elders of the capital village; under both Old Hop and Standing Turkey, the capital was Echota. The persons and roles within this body were like those of the body of elders of any Cherokee village. There was the village priest chief (first Old Hop, then Standing Turkey), his three major priest assistants, the village speaker, the village council of seven clansmen, and the remaining beloved men of Echota. The remainder of the Echota villagers gathered as clansmen. All Cherokee villages were represented as political units. Each village sent its priest chief, his right hand man, his messenger, and usually also some members of the village council of clansmen and others who desired to attend. These tribal councils were held in conjunction with the religious ceremonies of the New Year. The ceremonies of the capital village were performed by the body of Echota elders and were attended by the representatives of all the villages and by any others who so desired.[48]

The tribal organization for war was less structured. There was a tribal war chief from the capital village. War parties were often voluntary associations of young men from the villages, but sometimes under the central leadership as during the war with South Carolina, when the war activities were under the direction of the tribal war chief from the capital village Echota. Warriors with special talents, such as Little Carpenter, carried on the negotiations with foreign powers under directives from Echota.

A description of the tribe at this point in terms of its structural poses would be but slightly more complicated than describing the villages. Two of its poses, for household affairs and clan revenge, depict an aggregate of villages operating independently; each village was ordered by household and clan section, as described in Chapter 1, with the slight additional complication of the random web of kin ties among villages.[49] What was before a single pose for village councils becomes now two. In respect to domestic political matters (e.g., care of public buildings, or a decision to move), villages appear still to have been independent, hence the tribe may be drawn as an aggregate of villages, each organized in the usual village manner for council. Public policy in foreign affairs, on the other hand, was the large political necessity faced by the tribe as a body, and the priest state for that purpose may be seen as, in part, the tribal council outlined above. Similarly, what was once the nominal village structure for war becomes two. For ballplays, the villages probably still acted independently as before. For the implementation of foreign affairs, however, the tribe was nominally ordered by the tribal war organization. Such a description of the tribe suggests, then, six poses, only slightly more complicated by one additional fact. During tribal councils, the total tribal population was not involved; those at home, depending on what occupied them, could have been ordered as households or clans, but it is not likely that they would be found ordered by the pose for council or war. (The structural pose for tribal council is schematically represented in Figure 7.)

The degree of success of Old Hop's government is difficult to measure accurately, but it must have been large. Old Hop's government was apparently able, even early in its existence, to arrive at a definite decision; in July, 1753, a Cherokee delegation left Echota for Charles Town with a clear directive (Logan 1859:460–81). Throughout the period, trade was never adequate judging from the almost incessant pleas sent to Charles Town and Williamsburg, and it was greatly reduced at times; however, it never stopped, and timely gifts of arms were frequent. In 1755, the war with the Creeks was successfully concluded with the battle of Taliwa which won for the Cherokees territory in northern Georgia (Mooney 1900:384–85). Early in 1756, Cherokee negotiators, aided by considerations connected with the approaching war with France (declared in May), induced South Carolina, Virginia, and North Carolina to build forts in the Overhills area (Williams 1937:152; Jenkins 1949:October 14 1755). From time to time, villages raided the English frontier; but Old Hop always managed to soothe the temper of these villages and of the English and prevented more serious consequences. Tellico made an open move to join the French but was checked. Whether raids by the French tribes could have been less frequent and less damaging is impossible to say; but Old Hop was never without messengers among some of them, especially the Shawnee, and

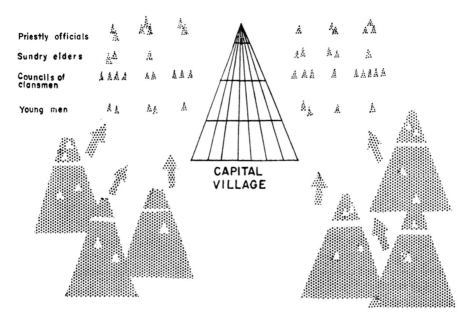

Priestly officials

Sundry elders

Councils of clansmen

Young men

CAPITAL
VILLAGE

FIG. 7. The structural pose of the Cherokee tribe for councils, 1750's.

there was a steady stream through Echota of emissaries from the tribes in French territory. Old Hop's government enjoyed a measure of success; it did, that is, up to May, 1759 when affairs simply fell apart and war followed.

From 1753 to May, 1759, tribal responsibility for the actions of any Cherokee became intensely evident. Twice in 1753, South Carolina demanded of the tribe that Cherokee individuals be turned over for punishment. Again in 1759, the same demand was made. In 1753, South Carolina pressed the tribe to stop hostilities against the Creeks, and, from 1756 on, there was the constant demand that war parties be restrained from raiding encroaching settlers. The constant threat was that trade would be cut off. In view of the ongoing, intense raids by French-allied tribes, the loss of a constant supply of arms could be expected to bring about the destruction of Cherokee villages in the outlying areas. The tribe could avert this danger only so long as every Cherokee refrained from the actions which South Carolina deemed punishable. Essentially this meant that warriors were not to molest traders and raid frontiers.

To restrain the young men required two things: a wise public policy in respect to relations with the colonies; and some means, once policy was set, to assure that young men abided by that policy. The roles and persons of the tribal priest state, although imperfect, seem to have been almost adequate to the first, but not yet adequate to the second.

In the formation of tribal policy, the young men appear to have been no problem. The sanctions associated with kin relations in the villages could be called upon by the old men. On the tribal level, as before in the villages, the crucial problem in forming policy was to achieve unanimity among the old men; the young could be readily enough brought into line.

It seems reasonably clear that unanimity was required on the tribal level as before, and it is very clear that achieving unanimity was more difficult.

The necessity of unanimity is suggested by observations of Ludovic Grant (1909:64), a trader intimately knowledgeable of Cherokees, who wrote of events in 1754:

Since I have been at Saludy and saw them give up their lands there I am persuaded it was because old Hop wanted to do it himself in the presence of all his people, and it is very happy that it was not done at that meeting at Chotte . . . [because] the Nation would never have thought it so binding upon them nor would they have been so generally pleased with it Whereas being done in a formal manner at Saludy and in the presence of all the headmen & head Warriors. . . . There is not one person in the whole nation who is not pleased with it.

Similarly, a colonial official argued, in 1754 (Willis 1955:229), that agreements with delegations in colonial capitals had no validity because the consent of the whole tribe was necessary. Finally, the priestly officials of the tribal state seem to have refrained from overbearing behavior as strongly as village priests, and probably for the same reason. Payne (MS, I:75) reported: "It has been universally remarked that nothing could be more urbane than the bearing of the Cherokee at these festivals. There was no loftiness, no sourness, no affectation; they were considerate to all . . . ." (Note that this refers to behavior during ceremonies, not councils proper; the same persons, however, are involved.)

The priest-state, because of its very structure, could not, as dependably as the villages, bring about a single, clear sentiment among all the old men throughout the tribe. In the villages, councils proceeded by a continual interchange among the old men of each of the village clan sections. All villagers were physically present in the councilhouse. The several opinions would form, the contrasts among them could be made known, and the old men who initially formed the several opinions could there and then modify them. Ultimately a unanimous sentiment was brought about, or no decision at all. In tribal councils this full interchange among those present was possible and appears to have been required. But not all old men were involved, only those present in the capital. The old men of a village might have formed a sentiment in a village council; their spokesmen at tribal councils presumably would express that sentiment. But modifications would necessarily have to be made by the village spokesmen, acting for the village; modification of that sentiment could not be made by all the village elders themselves. The delegation of such responsibility was new in Cherokee life; undoubtedly, many felt much less strongly bound than others by judgments so reached.

Achieving an effective decision was difficult for a second reason: men or groups who disagreed with crystallized sentiment could not, now, be allowed to drop out and then act as they pleased, for the main task was to prevent *all* raids. In the villages, there was no set of kinship statuses, or other persons, which could operate systematically among the old men so that some of them could exert coercion on others. Nor did such persons now come into existence.

In the villages, the implication was that councils worked circumspectly toward unanimity, some men perhaps disassociating themselves along the way. The appearance is equally strong that in tribal councils the old men circumspectly worked toward unanimity. But disassociating oneself or one's village did not carry with it license to raid, and men wishing that course would doubtless be less willing to cease their voiced objections.

Still, the record of the troublesome years from 1753 to May of 1759, suggests that Old Hop in spite of the unperfected, incompletely institutionalized structure, somehow generated and maintained an adequate measure of public sentiment. The Tellico incident reported was the most clear instance of one village standing in open contempt of others, but that stand was modified within 10 months. It seems probable that, given the degree of structural inadequacy suggested, it was only because of Old Hop's political talents (perhaps genius) that the tribe could create and maintain a measure of unified tribal sentiment adequate to forming tribal policy. The tribal structure of itself did not provide assurance that public policy for controlling the young men would be established with perfect firmness; but that policy was established, with some measure of perfection.

Perfectly firm and wise policy would not, in any event, have solved the problem of actually preventing the young men from raiding the frontier. The remarkable fact is that unauthorized raiding was held within manageable proportions. The villages, as we saw, had no real control over the young men once they were outside. The first quasi-governments could only punish and redress. No new persons or roles were created in the tribal war organization to enable it, as an administrative arm of the priest state, to do more.

The priest-state could send warriors to punish other warriors for some desired end. The tribal war organization, like the earlier governments, did use direct coercion. In 1753, a Cherokee from Kituhwa killed an English trader. Relations with England were extremely delicate at the time. There followed a number of councils among tribal and village officials and between some of those officials and South Carolina, all aimed at preventing English retaliation. Finally a group of warriors from the killer's village and neighboring villages searched out the killer and shot him (Jenkins 1949: February 19, 1754). In 1759 South Carolina demanded that 24 Cherokees be turned over as punishment for depredations on the frontier. There followed a similar, but less successful, attempt at coercion (Milling 1940:186-202). But these devices could only punish; the necessity was to prevent. For this, there was no means.

One is led to infer that the success of the Old Hop government in implementing policy, until May, 1759, was in large part due to the great energy and skill of Old Hop himself and others around him, operating often without the assistance of structural devices. When Old Hop became old and weak, affairs became even more complex, possibly even unmanageable by any structure with any amount of talent to draw on. In May, 1759, affairs got out of hand; raids on the frontier erupted; full war ensued. The priest-state had not been able to prevent the Cherokee actions which brought on the war.

With war, the loss of trade which had been feared occurred. And with war, the tribe experienced a more severe and very tangible kind of damage: in 1760, and again in 1761, villages and crops were burned by colonial military. The suffering occasioned by this kind of warfare probably brought about a strong (though less than universal) sentiment for peace. The tribal war chief himself, Great Warrior, "took Pity" on the women and children and worked consistently to restore and preserve peace for the rest of his life (Candler 1904–1916, IX: 77–78). The failure of the priest-state to prevent war did not immediately result in a change of its structure.

On the heels of Cherokee defeat, white settlers encroached more boldly on the land (Saunders 1886–1870, VII: 108–10). These encroachments increased the likelihood of retaliatory raids and hence the danger of a new loss of trade and new war. Because of the recent failure of the priest-state and because of the new threat, the beginnings of a shift in the Cherokee attitude toward coercive sanctions would soon appear. In effect, new sentiment was to form—a sentiment which favored some means of decent physical coercion by tribal officials to prevent those acts which would cut off trade or bring war with the English.

In sum, tribal structures for punishing wrongs began to appear in 1730, and a full structure to permit the forming of tribal public policy and to implement that policy emerged in the 1750's. This tribal priest-state appears to have been structurally inadequate for forming a strong sentiment among all the old men of the tribe; this inadequacy, it appears, was somehow overcome by the political talents of influential men. It was structurally still more inadequate to prevent raids on the frontiers and trading posts by the warriors; this inadequacy was less well overcome by talent, and this failure the Cherokees could not afford. Beyond that, Cherokee foreign relations were complex and were changing rapidly. For that combination of reasons, in 1760, the Cherokees fell into open war with South Carolina which lasted two and one-half years. During the war years, Old Hop died, and his place was filled by Standing Turkey, an old priest of the capital village, Echota. Following the peace, there were another two and one-half years of great and incessant pressures by encroaching settlers on Cherokee lands. The inability of the priest-state adequately to control the warriors set the stage for a basic change in the organization of the tribal state.

Moytoy's government was a replica of the village war organization. Old Hop's government duplicated, in addition, village structures for council. These duplications are not illumined by imagining custom to be dead weight of habit. Rather, village politics created working social systems: structures (more or less complete) and appropriate kinds of leading men, selected and trained, with taste and talent for the tasks involved. The tribe did not go to Moytoy: Moytoy and the Tellico men around him started doing the tribe's work, and the tribe came to accede. Old Hop and the Echota elders around him started doing the tribe's more difficult work—forming and expressing tribal sentiment —and the tribe came to accede. Both men were parts of on-going village systems: structures with men in them in working relation one to the other, men able and, for unknown reasons, willing to do the tribal work which arose.

CHAPTER 9

From Priests to Warriors: 1761-1775

THIS chapter traces the introduction into tribal politics of new kinds of coercion. Increased pressures by English settlers on Cherokee land heightened the danger of unauthorized raiding, hence of war. By 1768 the tribe appears to have accepted a new form of direct physical coercion in tribal life: the tribe brought the prominent warriors—as warriors—into tribal councils.

Before, during tribal councils, retired prominent warriors were simply old men among other old men. Before, the authority among war leaders was not structurally allowed except when the warriors were actually doing war work. Now, in tribal councils, war officials and prominent ex-warriors came to be seated together. This seating reflected a structural shift which brought to tribal affairs a coercion that was new in two senses: the physically coercive war relations were constantly and automatically available during both the forming of policy and its implementation; also, these coercive relations were becoming less an acultural pecking order and more a legitimate exercise of proper roles among recognized persons.

In 1761, the war ended. Standing Turkey was the tribal priest chief. During the next six or seven years new structuring with new coercion was introduced to tribal politics. Then the structure for tribal politics held steady through 1775.

No decisive events mark these years. The major threat to peace was the steady encroachment of settlers on Cherokee lands. On October 7, 1763, George III, recently ascended to the English throne, made a proclamation forbidding individuals to purchase Indian lands and forbidding settling on those lands; but settlers continued to press forward. At every occasion, tribal negotiators demanded the removal of intruders. They often received promises; these were sometimes fulfilled, but the relief was always temporary. With monotonous repetition in the years through 1775, colonial governments attempted to legalize the encroachments by purchasing those illegally settled lands from the tribe. Equally regularly, the Cherokees attempted to keep the peace by agreeing to the sales; they made the first of at least seven cessions in October, 1765 (Saunders 1886-90, VII:115-17).[50]

Still, tribal sentiment, as expressed by tribal officials, remained firmly against armed reprisals. Beginning in 1730, during 23 years, the tribe had turned over one Cherokee to South Carolina to be punished and had killed another Cherokee at South Carolina's insistence. In the 12 years since Old Hop, that extreme coercion had been exercized on two new occasions. Now, in a letter of November 19, 1761, there is evidence of serious intent to make even greater use of punitive sanctions. The tribal priest chief, Standing Turkey, wrote: "We are now Building a Strong House, and the very first of our People, that does any dammage to the English, shall be put in there, until the English fetch them . . . ." (Williams 1937:267–68). In 1763, Little Carpenter (Clark 1895–1905, XI:156–203), at a conference of several southeastern tribes, told what Cherokee government policy would be: " . . . the beloved Headman of Choti sits under a White Flag and wishes to preserve it from Blood and any one who may make it otherwise will be found out . . . ."

Moreover, prominent warriors seem to have begun somehow to exercise control over the young men. In 1765, a prominent Overhills warrior and associate of Great Warrior, the tribal war chief, spoke very firmly to a group of young men of the Lower section who were grumbling over the recent cession of land: "Do not say you do not know where the new boundary is," he told them, and " . . . don't shame your Warriors any more by letting them hear you have stolen horses or burnt woods or made disorder . . . . [We] are tired travelling backwards and forwards to make up matters for you" (Saunders 1886–90, VII:115–17). Without firm restraints recurrent incidents might have led to war. In 1766, a Creek was seeking Cherokee warriors to join him in attacks on the frontier (Saunders 1886–90, VII:209–10). Other war parties from the Algonkian speaking tribes to the north who would welcome support were constantly passing through Cherokee country on the way to the frontier (Saunders 1886–90, VII:256–57). That same year, five Cherokees were killed in Virginia; anger was high for months, but no revenge party went out (Saunders 1886–90, VII:210–11). And Cherokee hunters constantly came across encroaching white men in their hunting territory, but no serious conflicts occurred.

Only a few leaders imposed restraints, and although the legitimacy of that restraint was not yet clearly established, the measures taken were publicly approved. Apparently the force worked. None of the provoking events led to Cherokee raids on the frontier and there was no war. This cumulative experience probably went far to demonstrate to Cherokees at large that this specific kind of coercion in tribal affairs was desirable.

This shift in public sentiment appears to have taken place during six or seven years following 1761. By 1768, Great Warrior, the tribal war chief, became the "tribal chief" and took over the political functions of the tribal priest chief. Great Warrior's assumption of the priest chief's political work, and the larger structural change and shift in sentiment it appears to reflect, did not occur suddenly. In 1763, Standing Turkey died. Great Warrior, now in his sixties, attempted immediately to step into the tribal priest chief's place. On May 21, 1763, he wrote to the Governor of Georgia, " . . . you are Governour of Georgia and I of the Cherokees" and signed "Oconastota, King and Governour of the Cherokee Indians" (Candler 1904–16, X:77–78). That first bid was temporary and for four years the top position in tribal government was unclear, two or three persons being variously named. But in October of 1768, Great Warrior was the principal signer of a treaty (Saunders 1886–90, VII:851–55), and from that time on he was named by observers, with almost perfect consistency, as the tribal chief.

Sometime during those four years, public sentiment had shifted to accept the warriors in tribal deliberations. Bartram (1854:21–34) visited the Cherokees and other southeastern tribes and recorded a generalized description of tribal councils throughout the area.[51] He describes a structure in part similar to the structure under Old Hop. A priestly "king" with at least one assistant sat in councils "at the head of chiefs of tribes and families [read: the village representatives and the capital body of elders]." There were also a war chief and a war priest. But he describes a seating arrangement[52] which appears significantly to contrast with the seating in the villages and under Old Hop. According to Bartram, the war chief sat during councils, at the head of the old and famous warriors. He went on to single out the war priest as "a person of great power and consequence in the state." The old warriors appear to have begun to act in councils as a recognized group.

The structural changes, seen as the coming to be of new persons, is impossible to depict in detail because the data are too thin. In councils, it appears, the set of persons did not become greatly more complicated than in the government of Old Hop. Probably, the person of tribal chief was viewed as a new niche, emerging with Great Warrior and not supplanting the older tribal priest chief (whose role, however, would have changed). Beyond that, new persons among the elders were created to provide distinct niches for prominent ex-warriors in contrast to others who had not so distinguished themselves. Persons of the current war chief and war priest were new only in the context of councils. Presumably the persons of the young men, sorted as to village, remained unchanged. About the tribal war organization, as new or modified persons, nothing can be said.

All too few data are available concerning roles in the emergent social structure. We cannot safely speak about the role behavior expected of tribal chief in his relations with elders and warrior-elders during councils; we may suggest that such a role, played for the first time and, so far, by only one man, be considered uninstitutionalized as yet. There is no reason to assume any new features in the role behavior expected among those elders who were not old and prominent warriors. Circumspect conduct was probably still recommended. This, we saw, was in some measure a structural imperfection, but, assuming talent on the part of the political leaders, the tribe seems not to have required greater perfection.

The roles of the old warriors were the important, new features of tribal councils. When the prominent old warriors came into the council they brought with them their accustomed set of war relationships. In part, these were acultural; in part, as among war officials, they were institutionalized roles. In both respects these relations were coercive. It is necessary to recall that toward warring and prominent warriors, Cherokees had had mixed feelings; these sentiments were expressed through a set of customs, including ritual purification after war and the exclusion of warriors as warriors from the two closely related events, ceremonies and most councils, events which were regarded by Cherokees as the clearest expression of the good life. Much of the mystique surrounding ceremonies and councils, earlier in the villages and now in the tribal body, dealt with discovering and keeping on "the white path," with the survival of the Cherokees and with maintaining their moral place in the harmony of men and nature. Warriors had become necessary to that grand design. Bringing warriors into council probably reflected and helped crystallize the public sense that a warrior career had become an unambiguous and integral part of the good life. I suggest that, as war careers became newly evaluated in this way, the conditions were set which necessarily would soon make of the *de facto* coercive relations among warriors some systematic set of roles, with exact recommendations for acceptable coercive conduct. I do not imagine that, in the period under consideration, this had yet occurred; it was still in process.

In the tribal war organization, viewed as an administrative arm of the council, no new persons were apparent. However, it is very likely that in the system of roles there were changes. The organization included the newly honored war officials. The presumption is strong that, as above, when Cherokees made warring and warriors an unambiguous part of the good life, that created conditions which allowed and assisted the institutionalization of the coercive roles throughout the war organization.

I have reviewed changes which began in 1761. During the following six or seven years there developed an increasing public recognition of the necessity for new physical coercion in tribal government; this resulted, by 1768, in bringing the warriors as warriors into council. That change set the conditions for further change—the greater institutionalization of war relations through the creation of legitimate and more precise war roles to replace the acultural pecking order among warriors. But that development was to be cut short.

For a complex of reasons, the creative process under way did not long continue. Increasing pressures on the land plus events in the colonies soon made it impossible for the old men with the old war leaders to restrain the young, and in 1776 a tribal schism occurred. After the schism there was a reaction and the priests replaced the old warriors in the major positions in tribal government. Tribal affairs were by then so greatly disorganized that any judgment about the use of the new force by the priests or by others on request of the priests is impossible. Shortly, the priest-state was dead.

In 1774, two events occurred which, each in its way, led directly to the tribal schism of 1776. In 1774, Daniel Boone, in the employ of a real estate company, explored the northern part of the Cherokee hunting territories, now Kentucky. That same year, the citizens of Boston dumped English tea into the harbor. Daniel Boone's explorations proved that an ambitious scheme to open Kentucky for settlement was feasible. In 1775, the engineers of the plan called Cherokee officials to a meeting at Sycamore Shoals and there proposed to buy Kentucky. Great Warrior, the Little Carpenter, Old Tassell, and other influential old men yielded to the pressure. The Little Carpenter's son, Dragging Canoe, a young warrior, opposed it. The old men signed the agreement; Dragging Canoe swore he would kill any settlers (Brown 1938:9–10). One month later, the Battle of Lexington opened the American Revolution. The frontier settlers were, by and large, rebels; loyalists would arm Dragging Canoe to kill rebels. Thus Dragging Canoe and the young warriors who were gathering around him were assured a source of arms. In June, 1776, the first raids on the frontier began. The English agent to the Cherokees wrote of the days just before this attack (Saunders 1886–90, X:778–79):

Almost all the young warriors from the different parts of the Nation followed [Dragging Canoe's] example. . . . But the principle Chiefs, who were averse to the measure and remembered the Calamities brought on their Nation by the last war, instead of opposing the rashness of the young people with spirit, sat down dejected and silent.

Through the summer, the Americans fought against the Cherokees and burned virtually every Cherokee house. The old men continued in their attempts to stop the war. By January, 1777, Dragging Canoe and his followers had withdrawn from their home villages and established new settlements farther south, separated from the rest of the tribe. These new villages came to be called the Chicamaugas.

The schism broke the union between the young warriors and the prominent ex-warriors. The tribe separated along the line of the age status cleavage. The old priests, the old retired war leaders, and the village war chiefs stayed in their home villages. Many of the young warriors, with their wives and children, went with Dragging Canoe.

The old men who remained probably attempted to re-establish the structure of Old Hop. In 1775, Great Warrior, because of his age, had resigned. Old Tassell was his successor. Old Tassell, like Old Hop and Standing Turkey, was a beloved man with no previous notoriety as a warrior. The religious festivals continued, probably under the direction of Old Tassell and the priests he drew around him. However, with Old Tassell, the capital village shifted for the first time since Old Hop's period of office from Echota; the new capital was Old Tassell's home, Toquo.

But Old Tassell's government was doomed from the start. From his first important official act on the negotiating of a peace treaty in May, 1777, Old Tassell's government could speak only for the Overhills area; after signing the treaty, they made a talk to the Lower and Middle villages, requesting them to take similar action, but without result. Dragging Canoe had located to the south and was directing raids against the Kentucky area to the north. His raiding parties passed through Old Tassell's country followed often by parties of White militia in pursuit. Considerable numbers of the younger men from villages under Old Tassell joined Dragging Canoe's war parties as they passed; and White militia did not or could not always distinguish Cherokee enemy from Cherokee friend.

The war between the Chicamauga Cherokees and the Americans kept the Old Tassell government in a constant state of crisis. Very shortly, pervasive effects were apparent in the organization of tribal government. To Buttrick's informants, the 1780's marked the end of the old ways. From then on, councils were no longer opened with prayer (Payne MS, III:22). The six major festivals telescoped eventually into one: the Green Corn Festival. By the mid 1780's, the festivals were wholly affairs of each village acting independently; before, there had been the great festivals in the capital village and, at least in the case of the Green Corn Festival, following them the tribal council had given a signal for all the villages to begin simultaneously their several festivals (Payne MS, III:89). Mooney's informants (Mooney 1900:257) pointed to the same decade as the time when the last great medicine men [read: priests] died.

Among the Chicamaugas, where the young warriors were freed from the restraint of the old beloved men, fearsome men directed the fearful, the strong governed the weak. The villages were almost devoid of ceremony, humane restraint was at a minimum, there was no effective wise leadership. Probably, the Chicamaugas experienced, as nearly as any human group has, the law of the jungle.

The divided Cherokees slipped into virtual anarchy. In the villages of Old Tassell, there were amiable old men; in the Chicamaugas, violent young men. The old men saw their priestly government crumble; the young men had thrown the political structure away. Neither one found an adequate substitute.

An assessment of the adequacy of the tribal political structure, modified during the time of Great Warrior, must focus on the central political necessity: to control the young men, and thereby to preserve the peace. The village political systems had no devices adequate to that task, nor had the early forms of the tribal political system. Cherokees perceived that they could no longer afford rampages outside the tribe by the young men, but they had not yet devised the means of control.

The changes required were not in the council structure, which had been an imperfect but, assuming talent on the part of the leaders, an adequate system of influence since Old Hop. It was the highly inadequate system of authority in the war organization which required modification. The record shows that changes were made in the structure of the council, but those changes had effects of functional significance for the war organization. The essence of the changes appears to have been as follows: The prominent warriors were brought into council; this marked warring as a fully acceptable avenue of the good life; conditions were now set for the institutionalization of coercive sanctions as part of the tribal system of authority; a means adequate for preventing raids had been developed. In short, these structural changes armed with public support the only men who in fact could prevent the young men from raiding, the war leaders.

Note that the narrow notion of ethos used in this study makes possible such a chain of inference. Ethos was taken to mean moral virtuosity—a goal to work toward, not to be achieved by all, but, to the degree achieved, rewarded. A basic change in the Cherokee ethos so understood has become apparent. Before, there was one recommended course for the good life; now there appeared a second, alternative course.

I deal with culture at its growing tip. Moreover, that tip was shortly to be cut off. It follows that the things which can be said as to the adequacy of this structure admit of no important measure of empirical proof. The data which bear on the matter are already put down. I briefly point up certain items.

I was not able to say, from the data, that the warrior-elders properly held greater influence in council than elders not warriors. That these were distinguished as persons seems clear, but the rank of their respective roles is totally unclear. However, considering the need for solving the central political problem, the control of the young men, it is reasonable to believe that regardless of role definition the warrior-elders enjoyed the larger influence in council. Policies thrashed out among the warrior-elders would be enforceable, whatever the others might feel.

It was, however, a matter of some importance that an appearance of singleness of purpose be achieved in council. The crucial work of the council was both to express and create tribal cohesion, and the tribal interests were under incessant attack. The newly modified system of persons and roles gives no strong indication that it could reliably bring about that cohesion. But that system was still in process of formation, hence the data are difficult to assess.

We may turn from the person axis for a moment, to take up the notion of individual, and the notions which seemed indicated when we asked earlier about kinds of Cherokee men. We found reason to expect among war officials aggressive men but men also with self-awareness and control. Great Warrior could have been suggested as a datum: a man of much singleness of purpose, often willful, covered with war scars, but a man famous for never having lost a warrior in battle. One may imagine such a man summoning his self-control and working adequately with warrior-elders and elders not warriors and, with some measure of circumspection, pressing firmly for cohesion among the council, hence among the tribe.

I am suggesting that the modified tribal council was in the nature of a compromise. One gets a sense of workability of the council in such an emergent period by having asked what kind of men were doing the work, in some measure without structural devices.

One may also imagine what it would be like to be a young man, to whom war is congenial, living in the context of the traditional Cherokee ethos; one may then note the changes in the ethos implied by the ex-warriors coming into council and ask: would this make a difference? My feeling is compellingly that it would. Now was opened up a second road to full repute. A young man was already somewhere along that road. There in council stood the men to emulate, the prominent ex-warriors. There, too, were the men who could assist a young man along the way, the war officials, who wielded authority during the activities of war parties. My feeling is that a young man to whom war was congenial could not fail to see himself in a new light and see the war officials in a new light. Both of these revised images established necessary conditions, traditionally absent in Cherokee life, for the institutionalization of war roles. Such emergent roles would seem to have increased the effective authority of prominent warriors over others younger and less prominent. But all this, in the Cherokee instance, is beyond proof.

CHAPTER 10

The Rise of Voluntary, Naive States

THIS brief chapter suggests that there is in the world a recurrent phenomenon, a process of state formation to be called here the "Mesopotamian"
career to statehood.[53]

I have outlined the features of the political system which characterized the
Cherokee village, and shall say that the same features seem to have characterized also the precivilized Mesopotamian village. Such a set of features is often
to be found in various parts of the world. I suggest that such a village political
system uniquely equips a people to begin one process of state-formation.

The rise of the Cherokee state in the mid-1700's was one instance of independent face-to-face communities voluntarily becoming a state; I have described the creation of that state. The rise of the earliest states in what became
Mesopotamia was probably another instance. It seems probable that this voluntary process, once begun, follows a characteristic career.

In human history, probably thousands of states have been created by an
unending process; states are formed, then break up into parts (perhaps joined
by parts from other states similarly broken), and reorganize themselves into
new states. The formation of the United States was an instance of the creation
of a state out of parts, each part having had in its political tradition the prior
experience of statehood.

But in some few score instances in human history, states have been formed
by people who have had no prior experience of living in states. These new or
naive states may arise through the conquest or forceful dominance of one community over others. Or these naive states may arise voluntarily, as when several politically independent face-to-face communities join as a single state.

I deal here with the building of voluntary, naive states and suggest that
the career called here Mesopotamian is one route by which such states are
formed, perhaps the only route.

The Cherokee village political system had five essential features. First, the
villagers consciously distinguished between two categories of core political
tasks: one category was coordinated through voluntary consensus, the second
through a hierarchy of command. Second, the villagers sorted themselves as
personnel differently for the two sets of tasks, that is, they employed two
structural poses; persons in the personnel arrangement for the tasks coordinated through consensus were constrained to use as a major sanction the
withdrawal of affection or, in the extreme, ostracism, while persons in the
hierarchy of command employed physical force and the threat of such coercion.
Third, the villagers raised different individuals to positions of leadership in
the two systems of personnel. Fourth, villagers selected those two kinds of

106

leaders on the basis of their respective competences as demonstrated in past performance; leadership was primarily achieved, not ascribed by birth; the salient, required qualities were, for the tasks coordinated through consensus, restrained sensitivity to nuances of feeling in others, and, for the command tasks, fearless and egocentric courage. And fifth, the village offered a greater honor to those restrained and sensitive persons who led in the tasks which required voluntary consensus.

These five features summarize the "white" and "red" tasks of Cherokee core politics, and the structural pose for each together with salient recruitment facts.

Jacobsen (1943) describes the precivilized Mesopotamian village by inference from the mythical social organization of the gods as depicted in the mythology of later civilized Mesopotamia. The parallels between the political organizations of the Cherokee village throughout the 18th century and the precivilized Mesopotamian village are similar enough to justify considering the two as belonging to a single class. The structure and procedure of general village councils—one category of political work for both peoples—appear virtually identical. The Cherokee village priest chief had a counterpart in a foremost elder suggested to Jacobsen by the god An (the father of the gods) in the Mesopotamian village council. The Cherokee body of elders had a Mesopotamian counterpart suggested by the body of 50 senior gods. In Mesopotamian councils, decisions were apparently reached by a semblance of unanimity very similar to decisions in Cherokee councils: Cherokees brought themselves into the deferential frame of mind appropriate to councils by holding councils in conjunction with religious festivals, while Mesopotamian villagers are said to have created euphoria before councils by drinking; in working toward decisions, Cherokee elders were the large influences and did the more difficult work, while the Mesopotamian elders "carried" the discussions; the Cherokees used magic to make their arguments in council irresistible, while Mesopotamian villagers seem to have prayed for the same power, and both admired the ability to be convincing; the Cherokees had to rely on the voluntary deference among the elders, while Mesopotamians called discussions "asking one another"; adequate agreement by a Cherokee was indicated by withholding further objections, and in precivilized Mesopotamia silence was consent; the Cherokee priest chief (or his speaker) announced the group decision as did a Mesopotamian counterpart. The implementation of decisions was alike: Cherokees were expected explicitly to step aside or, if they did not, to abide on their own accord by unanimous council decisions, and those who did not experienced the diffuse displeasure of the whole village; Mesopotamian village decisions were followed by a "promise," probably a self-binding vow, by all present.

As with the Cherokee "red" tasks, whenever a Mesopotamian village faced a crisis situation, especially war, it temporarily delegated power to a person selected to be "king" and the village became some hierarchy of command. (The particulars of the hierarchy Jacobsen does not describe; it would indeed be re-

markable if it turns out that the Mesopotamian hierarchy is obscure because
it was, like the Cherokee, partly acultural.)

Hence, for both Cherokees and Mesopotamians, there seem to have been
two categories of village tasks. To accomplish the two kinds of task, there apparently were two systems of personnel. One system operated through a chain
of command with powers to punish, the other through a gradation of influence
which depended primarily on the sanction of withdrawing affection. It follows
that the art of leadership was, in each system, very different.

In Cherokee village politics we found that any man could aspire to leadership in either system. Leaders seem to have been selected on the basis of age
and demonstrated competence. "Red" leadership fell to young men and the
"white" leadership fell to old men, so a man could have become prominent in
both systems at different points in his life—but almost none did. The Cherokee
political system selected out two kinds of men with two kinds of competence.
A leader in red tasks rose in the war ranks through success at war which included artful operation within the hierarchical system of commanders and
commanded. The kind of man who emerged at the top was egocentric, fear-inspiring, often termed "mean." These men were given formal honors and
sometimes material rewards; but otherwise they were held at arm's length,
often greeted with suspicion or ambivalence. A leader in Cherokee white tasks
emerged by the gradual accumulation of affection through most of a lifetime.
This man was circumspect and sensitive to the sentiments, often unspoken or
indirectly and ambiguously spoken, of those around him. Such men epitomized
the good man; they enjoyed unmixed respect and were called the beloved men.

It is unclear whether in Mesopotamian villages leadership was achieved
rather than ascribed, and whether the same persons rarely or often became
prominent in both systems of personnel. It is clear that leadership in those
tasks which were coordinated through consensus was more honorific than the
temporary leadership of the kings during crises.

These data, then, suggest that the political systems of Cherokee and
Mesopotamian villages appear identical in that both peoples distinguished between two categories of village tasks and both seem to have reorganized themselves as personnel for each category; I further suggested that there is some
possibility that Mesopotamian villages, like Cherokee villages, selected leaders
according to demonstrated competence rather than birth, and seldom raised
the same individual into prominence in both kinds of leadership, hence selected
for leadership different kinds of men. The data, finally, suggest that both
Cherokees and precivilized Mesopotamians awarded greater honor to the
leaders in those tasks coordinated through consensus, relative to the leaders
who were commanders.

This parallel, imperfect as the data are, strikes one as remarkable. One's
interest is further strengthened by the considerable possibility that this kind
of political system is not rare. Jacobsen suggests that the political organization of the precivilized Mesopotamian village was paralleled by the villages
of primitive Europe, particularly those of the Teutonic tribes and of Homeric

Greece, and by those of the Hittites (Jacobsen 1943:172 and n.). Very similar political systems seem characteristic of North American Indian groups as divergent as the Cheyenne (Llewellyn and Hoebel 1941), the Hopi (Titiev 1944), the Pueblos (Ellis 1951), and the Fox (Miller 1960). The features seem not to occur in Southeast Asia and probably not in Africa. In view of such wide distribution, this set of practices appears to be one stable form of political system which small face-to-face societies may frequently develop. Any society may qualify which has a peace chief and a war chief, or inside and outside chiefs, and which utilizes as its major sanction a loose form of ostracism.

From this base of village political system, the aggregate of Cherokee villages began a career which led to their tribal state.

The aggregate of Cherokee villages was, we saw, a jural community, a system of sovereign villages related to one another in a manner which systematically regulated the resolution of hostilities among villages.

Adams, in a brief paper on the common features of the careers to statehood in the Near East and Middle and South America, reports (1956:228):

> Our story begins in each region [including precivilized Mesopotamia] with an established network of agricultural communities, perhaps centering their socio-religious life around small shrines like those known for . . . the Early Ubaid of Mesopotamia. . . .

I listed above a number of peoples who seem to have the kind of political system found in Cherokee and Mesopotamian villages. Among these, it is very likely that the Cheyenne also formed a jural community; among sovereign Hopi villages and among them and some other Pueblo peoples there probably existed jural communities; the Fox had such relations with other Algonkian speaking peoples and probably, at certain post-Contact times, with the Iroquois confederacy. In all these instances shared ritual events (including mutual visiting to attend ceremonies) existed and probably gave form and mythical and emotional support to maintaining mutually restraining relations among independent sovereignties.[54]

Jural communities are probably a human universal and seem clearly to have existed among instances of the type of political system before us; from this it seems that the archeological evidence, ambiguous as that must be, permits the inference that this network of Mesopotamian villages was a jural community and that the relations among the villages were given specific form and support by common religious practice.

Cherokee villages began their career toward statehood under conditions of external duress; the recognized choice was statehood or pain.[55] The first moves toward statehood were explicitly in response to this new fact: persons in any village had no control over the behavior of other villages, and yet could be made to suffer because of that behavior.

Adams (1956:228) suggests the presence of external stress arising under different conditions in Mesopotamia. The first move toward statehood, he says, " . . . is perhaps most 'understandable' where irrigation or other systems of intensive cultivation requiring the planned efforts of sizeable groups were necessary and practical, as in southern Mesopotamia . . . ." Thus in the one instance a Cherokee villager might suffer from another Cherokee's raid on the Colonial frontier, while in the other a Mesopotamian might lose a crop and his family might starve through the action of another Mesopotamian upstream who clogged or destroyed the irrigation canal or the dike upon which they jointly depended.

Under such conditions, the first Cherokee moves toward statehood were coordinated by religious officials. These were leaders trained and selected with respect to proficiency in that class of village tasks traditionally coordinated through voluntary consensus; hence these first leaders were those who, among all villagers, were most circumspect, who enjoyed the most practiced sensitivity to the nuances of feeling in others—the moral virtuosos of village life. These men were able to move unthreateningly behind the territory-wide consensus they helped create. I have described the practiced patience and restrained qualities of Cherokee village priest chiefs. In the 1750's under such priests—first Old Hop, then Standing Turkey—the first Cherokee tribal state was formed.

Adams reports (1956:228):

. . . the formal integration of these communities [including the Mesopotamian villages] into areal groupings seems in each case first to have been achieved on a significant scale by individuals whose authority devolved from their positions as religious spokesmen . . . .

The Cherokee case has suggested reasons for the religious officials' success in guiding this process. The Cherokee village selected and trained a leadership especially gifted in sensing and forming public sentiment. Given the need to coordinate the actions of more than one village, this leadership was especially equipped to sense minute jealousies and to nurture trust. Under such leaders a cohesive public sentiment had the best possible chance to form. In the first decades of emergent voluntary states, the rate of collapse of state structures is probably very high. Possibly, where men so trained exist and where leadership falls to them, the hope of success is largest.

For both Mesopotamians and Cherokees, once the sovereign villages had formed their respective states, new forms of legitimate physical coercion soon appeared. Similarly for both, the men who were newly drawn into the center of the state systems to exercise the new forms of coercion were the war leaders, those men traditionally adept in the exercise of physical coercion in their relations with their fellows.

The parallel has to this point been remarkably close and suggests that we may be dealing with a recurrent type of social change, the Mesopotamian career to statehood.

The notion of structural pose helped identify two discreet systems of relations: two sets of persons and roles selecting two kinds of men adept at two kinds of political work. These systems have displayed remarkable adaptability under varying conditions from the original sovereign villages, through early forms of state and then later modifications. Many of the phenomena of social life are less enduring (for example kinship which shifted for most Cherokees to a bilateral system; on the other hand, it can plausibly be argued, the two systems we have been considering shortly became Cherokee political parties). The notion of structural pose appears to be a tool of some utility in identifying social phenomena which work with a measure of regularity.

From this point forward, however, the similarity between the two careers is limited. Now, each state introduces different forms of coercion. In the Cherokee case, the new coercion came about for long-standing reasons, those which caused the state to begin to emerge in 1730: the need for controlling the warriors outside of the village. That need was not met by Moytoy's nor (in institutionalized fashion) by Old Hop's government. In the period of Great Warrior's government the tribe was still trying to devise the controls.

In the Mesopotamian case, I imagine the original need (or one central need), to coordinate the handling of water, might have been met by the Mesopotamian equivalent of Old Hop's government. The farmers were, after all, in the village or close-by during the activity (as Cherokee warriors were not); if relatively firm state-wide sentiment as to handling water systems could be formed, as seems possible in that structure, the usual sanctions in the relations between old and young presumably could evoke adequate compliance.

But note what Adams observes (1956:229):

... forces inherent in temple control, some of them only coming into being in societies already integrated by temple leadership, gradually weakened the foundations on which temple supremacy rested. The increasing heterogeneity of society, for example, although largely a product at first of elaborations of the temple establishments, must have decreased the effectiveness of purely religious sanctions in the administration of community affairs. Warfare, previously confined mainly to raids, increased in scale and importance. . . .

Under the influence of all these forces the effective integration of communities in each of the areas required an increasingly authoritarian, militaristic, and centralized character that was also fundamentally in opposition to the traditional activities of the temple.

Heterogeneity did not make its appearance in the Cherokee case (there was no appreciable wealth, little specialization, and no social classes). Warfare increased in the Cherokee instance, but for very different reasons.

Adams' study included the classical first states in the Andes and in Middle America which, with Mesopotamia, followed the same career. I have no competence regarding the nature of the political systems of the precivilized villages in these New World areas, but perhaps these too began from the same village base (the later parallels make the presumption fairly strong) and are other instances of the Mesopotamian career to statehood. On the other hand, the Hopi, other Pueblos, Cheyenne, and Fox seem not to have set out upon any moves toward statehood.

This chapter has suggested that the social change called here the Meso-potamian career to statehood is a recurrent phenomenon, one route by which sovereign villages join voluntarily and naively to become states. The base for that career, the village political system described, is a frequently occurring form of political system. This career to statehood has occurred at least twice, and probably more often, in whole or in part, in widely separate areas.

The career itself could not be presented economically except with the aid of the notion of structural pose. The basic ingredient of the village political system was the two discrete sets of persons and roles, with two appropriate kinds of men, able to do two different kinds of political work. The subsequent permutations of those two systems tell the story of the rise of the Cherokee and Mesopotamian states.

Notes

[1] These population estimates are necessarily broad. Reports in the early 1700's contain total population estimates ranging from 10,000 to 20,000, and estimates of the number of settlements ranging from 53 to 64. The following materials contain census reports:

1715: Census totals from 60 settlements by South Carolina giving breakdown: men, women, children (Logan 1859:207).
1721: Census of 10 settlements by South Carolina giving breakdown: men, women, children for each settlement (Williams 1937:85–86).
1721: Estimate by South Carolina of the total population (Logan 1859:376–77).
1735: Report as to the number of villages and of warriors (Adair 1775:227).

Neither the location nor the number and size of the settlements held steady through the 18th century. At the beginning of the 1700's the Valley settlements were expanding slowly westward along the Hiwasee River at the expense of the Yuchi Indians. In 1738 there was a smallpox epidemic which was reported to have killed one half of the Cherokees. In the 1750's the Cherokees suffered intensive war losses: the Overhill settlements were under attack by Indians allied with the French, and the Lower villages were under more serious attack by Creeks and by South Carolina. Still, one outcome of those battles was a southward movement of Lower settlements into northern Georgia at the expense of the Creek. By the 1760's the Cherokee popultion was almost certainly less than 10,000, and a detailed report lists only 43 settlements (Bartram 1928:301–02).

[2] This third ceremony seems to have become incorporated into the harvest ceremony sometime during the last half of the 1700's (Payne MS, I:82).

[3] Some form of general amnesty for crimes against fellow villagers is widely but inconsistently reported as occurring at this ceremony. The Cherokees practiced clan revenge for murder and other injuries. It appears that amnesty was declared at this ceremony at least for unintentional killings and lesser injuries if still unrevenged (Haywood 1823:264).

[4] It follows that I judge that the "uncentralized" political systems as described by Fortes and Evans-Pritchard (1940), and Middleton and Tait (1958) are, in minor respects, wrongly described. The affairs which are ordered in these societies by segmentary lineage systems and other devices are, I judge, the foreign affairs of sovereign villages or districts.

[5] The materials for this chapter come, except for the few instances which will be noted, from the Payne-Buttrick manuscripts, Books I, II, III, IVa, and VIb. I shall not cite the particular Payne-Buttrick references except where special questions arise. I attempt to cite all of the few instances of testimony which run counter to interpretations made in these pages. We are indebted to the astute observation and questioning by the missionary Buttrick, especially so in areas of Cherokee life which are complex and less obvious to casual observation. All the other sources of 18th century Cherokee ethnography would, taken together, yield a very incomplete picture of the four structures of the Cherokee village. Buttrick's reports, with some little inference, do yield a full and plausible portrait of those structures. Two general sources of possible ethnographic error should be noted: first, Buttrick talked to old Cherokees in the 1830's about "the old days"; there was rampant historical change between the end of the period under consideration here (1775) and the 1830's, and other historical changes between 1700 and 1775; often these changes are ambiguously dated in these records. Second, Buttrick's informants talk mainly about the tribal organization, not the villages; following leads given by them as to parallels between the two, one can make reasonable inferences from the first to the second, but at some peril.

[6] I shall devote more attention to Cherokee roles in Chapters 2 and 3. The terminology here is close to Nadel's (1951), though I seem (I am not certain) to think of a larger proliferation of persons in any society; more significantly, I connect person to individual in a different way, as will be clear in Chapter 5.

[7] Few descriptions of social structure, in or following the British tradition, are couched in language which suggests that the thoughts of actors are the items described; the language sug-

gests that behavior is described. It is, however, self-evident that the mere existence of an imagined structural niche and of a recommendation for conduct does not guarantee that the appropriate men will at the appropriate time accept and act out that social thing; nor does it seem to help greatly to assert, as often is done, that most of the people most of the time act accordingly, and to assume that the exceptions do not bear importantly on the question at hand, usually the persistence of the society's structure. Among studies of social structural phenomena, it is easy to recognize when real behavior is actually being described: frequencies are counted and reported. When studies do not so report, they in effect describe ideas in the heads of members of the society, though they may imagine that they do otherwise. Firth (1954) and Leach (1954) explicitly treat social structure as normative ideas; Fortes (1945) and Evans-Pritchard (1940) do so implicitly.

[8] Gilbert (1943) has well described the total set of terms and relations among kindred. Certain of those relationships will be described in later chapters where they become crucial in village political behavior. I follow Gilbert's reports in all discussions of kinship in this study. Gilbert analyzed the Cherokee system as it existed in the 1930's in North Carolina. In the Payne manuscript, there are references to seven exogamous matrilineal clans (IVa:22), the levirate (III:35), incest rules forbidding marriage in one's own clan or one's father's clan. Although there are no 18th century descriptions of Cherokee kinship, the above facts are virtual proof that the Crow system described by Gilbert existed in the same essentials during the 1700's.

[9] The same term was probably applied to the children of one's wife's sisters, though Gilbert does not report a term for those relatives.

[10] That persons-with-roles have effects on behavior in contexts where they are thought not to apply is, of course, an evident human fact. In Chapter 5, I will suggest that such phenomena are best understood through studies ordered by the notion of individual. Only normative expectations are now put down.

[11] Note the contrast between this reordering of personnel and the reordering described in British studies of segmentary lineage systems. In the latter the phenomena of "nesting" is crucial: the set of persons operative at a lower level is subsumed by all higher levels so that minimal lineages are completely contained by medial lineages, and both by maximal lineages. I am describing one set of persons being made inoperative—temporarily obliterated—by another set. The difference is only partly ethnographic.

[12] Clans did not act as corporate units beyond the village boundary. Beyond the village, clans served as marriage classes and served other purposes described in Chapter 6. Lineages appear not to have acted corporately at any level.

[13] One Buttrick informant said one could not marry with individuals having "any blood connexions" (Payne MS, IVb:270).

[14] I deal here only with killings by a fellow villager. Clans were also required to seek blood revenge for warriors killed by enemy tribes; this was one item entering the deliberations of village council and war organization, and is mentioned in those contexts. Killings also occurred among Cherokees of different villages; that is considered in the context of the emergence of tribal government.

[15] Gilbert's two studies (1943, 1955) do not agree on the application of older brother and younger brother to lineage mates in the grandparental and grandchild generations; I follow here the later study.

[16] Priests and nonpriests were not classes of Cherokee society. A Buttrick informant (Payne MS, IVb:III) said of one of the four priestly officials: "I call this man a priest because he offered the sacrifices of the people, and was their intercessor with God. And in order to relieve him from all other cares, his field was tilled wholly by the town, and his family supplied, in part at least with corn." But virtually all Cherokee males from preadolescence on were students of priests, apprentices, assistants, and full-fledged practitioners, in that approximate order. Practitioners were differentiated from trainees, and that differentiation loosely coincided with the village system of age statuses; and among the practitioners there were differentiations as to the kinds of lore they knew and were called upon to practice. Priestly knowledge was hereditary "to a certain extent" (Payne MS, IVa:19). That extent probably was simply the tendency of priests to take as their apprentices the children of near relations, especially of their sisters. However, one Buttrick

informant stated without qualification that the office of the high priest was "hereditary, descending to the son, or in case the high priest had no son, to his highest male descendant" (Payne MS, IVb:322). (But see page 86 for an event which could be the source of that apparent error.) Sometimes a child was given in charge to a priest at birth but more often at the age of nine or ten. The child's training began soon after, as soon as he could understand. The training included occasional vigils with his teacher for 20 hours. A priest could have as many as seven pupils. Before a priest died, he selected one of his pupils to receive his religious paraphernalia.

[17] The set of rank and officialdom varies independently of the web of kinship excepting only the seven man war council which is based on clan membership. Hence, the total number of potential persons was the product of those two series, discounting only for the war council.

[18] I draw on Cherokee studies by several scholars working under the auspices of the Cross-Cultural Laboratory, Institute for Research in Social Science, University of North Carolina, as reported in preliminary papers by John Gulick whose full report is in preparation. I draw primarily on the inquiries of Robert K. Thomas (1958) as reported by John Gulick. Quotations are from two reports (Gulick 1958:27–29, and 1959:5–7). The Cherokee Conservatives form part of the Carolina Cherokee community. They are culturally conservative, that is, unacculturated relative to their nonconservative fellows, especially in respect to values. The Conservatives also tend to act as a minority political faction in Cherokee community affairs.

[19] Gulick interprets the presence of gossip and conjuring otherwise, as evidences of dysfunction in the harmony ethic under contemporary conditions.

[20] I have encountered no report of unusual amounts of gossip in the 1700's. The amount of magic seems much greater in the 18th century. If these be functional equivalents, the interesting interpretation suggests itself: as magic diminished (due perhaps to missionizing), the incidence of gossip rose.

[21] There were, however, ritual occasions when priests made moral preachments, sometimes lasting all day; there seems to be no equivalent among contemporary Cherokees.

[22] Cherokees in the 1700's seem to have had more ritual means to cope with potential conflict than do contemporary Cherokees.

[23] I shall make frequent use throughout the study of Jenkins' microfilm publication of South Carolina colonial documents. The pagination in the series is imperfect; however, the documents are filmed in approximate chronological sequence, hence I shall cite them by date.

[24] I draw again on Cherokee studies made under the auspices of the Cross-Cultural Laboratory, Institute for Research in Social Science, University of North Carolina, as those studies have been reported in a preliminary paper by John Gulick (1959).

[25] I have already shown that historical evidence indicates that the system of kinship *persons*, the Crow terminology, obtained then; I now make the unsupported assumption that the corresponding set of kinship *roles* likewise obtained then.

[26] It is perhaps instructive that, much later, in the early 1800's, when Cherokees were drawing constitutions and writing laws, this silence continues. The first constitutions say simply that delegates will be "chosen" and are silent as to how legislative bodies reach decisions.

[27] Gilbert alludes particularly to censuring the choice of a mate disallowed by incest laws; the presumption is that the right applied in other contexts. This and the following kinship data are taken from Gilbert (143:149–53).

[28] But note this passage from Timberlake (Williams 1927:109) which can be read to support or contradict: "Here is a lesson to Europe, two Indian chiefs, whom we call barbarians, rivals of power, heads of two opposite factions, warm in opposing one another, as their interests continually clash, yet these have no farther animosity, no family-quarrels or resentment. . . . "

[29] Birdwhistell (1952) knows how to describe many of these facts. We might also note that ethos in this meaning has closer affinity to personality than in other meanings; that is, if all roles tend to assume a common coloration, the suggestion is strong that they do so in response to modal personality factors.

[30] This is a particularly troublesome point in the Payne manuscripts. Buttrick asserts in his sundry letters to Payne, listed here in the order in which they were written, that: 1) the council decided on war (Payne MS, III:24), 2) the war chief and his right hand man (read: war priest)

decided, and the population acceded (Payne MS, III:58), and 3) the council decided (Payne MS, IVb:132–33). It is perhaps significant that in the second assertion, the motive given was to revenge Cherokee deaths; in the event of recent killings, the formal decision was usually nominal because of the clamor set up by relatives and clansmen who believed the deceased could not rest until his blood was revenged. In contrast, the first and third assertions begin: In case any of the chiefs apprehended danger . . . ; in that circumstance, true judgements were required.

[31] It is not likely that this is very similar to analogous phenomena in complex societies. Each of us is very many persons to very many others. But we usually succeed in keeping these in relatively small sets sealed off from one another (Goffman 1959:141ff.). The Cherokees were all of these at once. Probably, a close analogy is a suddenly swollen government bureau, or defense factory; and probably some of the same implications follow.

[32] All the above reports are from the later years of the 18th century. There are no clear descriptions by Europeans of behavior which apply clearly to warriors from the 1730's and 40's.

[33] Beginning in the 1730's, need was perceived for a tightening up in this area of Cherokee politics, and from that need flowed a series of innovations which will be the story of Part II of this study. This involved primarily intervillage coordination.

[34] Many British structuralists sometimes make this assumption explicitly, hence couch their reports in language which announces that real behavior is being described.

[35] One must make this probably false assumption in order to get on with the work. Ultimately, prediction appears impossible in respect to human behavior. The essential reason is that scientific understanding is public. In the usual run of affairs, that public understanding reaches the subjects, bringing with it new awareness of self or society, and basically altering the conditions under which the prediction was true. Accounting for "feed-back" seems not to solve the problem: one makes a new prediction, allowing for feedback from the first, but the second prediction then has its own effects on aware subjects, and so on. At least two qualifications are necessary: Where people don't care (as in electing between two brands of soap), predictions appear possible. And under certain conditions (as with the stock market) correct predictions are self-confirming. Polls are, of course, not predictions but summary descriptions. Nevertheless, the assumption that prediction is possible seems to make inquiry move in good directions.

[36] I should not pass on without listing recorded instances of resistance by the young men to that domination. All but two of these occurred in the context of war or negotiation.

Ludovic Grant (Jenkins 1949:February 8, 1754) wrote to South Carolina in 1754 reporting an extreme and rare inside-the-village instance of resistance to subordination. A warrior insulted the most respected beloved man of all the Cherokees of that time, saying he was an old women, was not a warrior and had never "given any proof thereof by killing his Enemy"; he threatened to beat the old man and forced him to flee the village. Milder disagreements tended to divide Cherokees along the line of age-status. A Buttrick informant reported (Payne MS, III:7):

> A difference of opinion now exists respecting the beginning of Spring and fall. Many years ago some of the young men asserted that February was the first month of Spring, but the old men contended that it was not, but that March was the first month. . . . The old men were highly displeased, and would not consent to this innovation.

Sub-rosa complaints by young war leaders were common during negotiations with the colonies. One was reported as early as 1716 (Willis 1955:212); a war leader complained to South Carolina officials that they "gave Ear to what [the beloved man] Characke Heaggy said & did not mind them." During hostilities in 1723, South Carolina officials observed (Willis 1955:233) that the old men were having difficulty controlling the young men. And, at the other end of my time period, Adair (1775:247) said, in reference to a flare-up of trouble between the Cherokee and English, that:

> . . . the hearts of their young warriors were so enraged, as to render their ears quite deaf to any remonstrance of their seniors, respecting an amicable accommodation [with the English].

[37] The separation of war from the rest of village life was also under-scored by a nonstructural fact, Cherokee color symbolism. War was symbolized by red, and peace by white. Timberlake (Williams 1927:62–3) observed:

... from this place I could take a view of the town [Settico], where I observed two standards of colours flying, one at the top, and the other at the door of the town-house; they were as large as a sheet, and white. Lest therefore I should take them for French, they took great care to inform me that their custom was to hoist red colours as an emblem of war; but white, as a token of peace. . . .

Buttrick reported (Payne MS, III:14) similar appositions of red and white. There was a red pole erected before the town house at times of war, and a white pole in times of peace. Black was also associated with war (Williams 1927:63–65).

[38] The phrase, "to challenge to ballplay" can connote "to declare war." Mooney (1900:377), recorded a myth about strife between two villages. At the climax of that enmity, a man from Cowee said to the assembled villagers of the other village: "Cowee will have a ball play with you" —and (the myth continues) everyone knew this was a challenge to battle.

[39] In the usual structural-functional studies, Cherokee councils, warfare, ritual purification, and ballplays (leaving aside ethos) would by this same logic be shown to be functionally interconnected. But note that this interconnection exists because the same young men experience all four activities, and that the interconnection is psychological in nature. However, structural studies let go of the experiencing individual and therefore include no systematic guarantee that two facts, between which such interconnection is imagined, are in fact experienced by the same men. This is a source of potential error. Probably such error is not often fallen into, because the axis of individual experience is somehow held in the mind. It seems apparent that such interconnection can only be shown on the individual axis, and that method ought to provide, if it can, built in guarantee against potential error.

[40] The materials are drawn from Jenkins (1949).

[11] There were surely many more than nine, but others do not appear in the record. Most recorders of Cherokee history were more likely to encounter war parties or negotiating delegations than old priests who usually stayed in their villages; when the priest chiefs were not individually known, they were often simply alluded to by office.

[42] I note the program of interdisciplinary comparative studies currently sponsored by the Social Science Research Council.

[43] I use jural community in the sense suggested by Middleton and Tait (1958:9).

[44] Fortes and Evans-Pritchard (1940) recommend the future comparison of centralized and "uncentralized" political systems. The peoples they term uncentralized are aggregates of sovereignties joined as jural communities. One compares, then, a single sovereignty (a "centralized" people) with an aggregate of sovereignties joined in a jural community (an "uncentralized" people). In all human instances there are sovereignties and jural communities. It seems reasonable to suppose that it is better to compare the commensurate levels of the respective systems. For the Cherokees, these levels of political organization have been identified by core political phenomena alone. Groupings wider than a sovereignty may act as a single organized unit in ritual events. It is an interesting comparative question whether the boundary of a sovereignty coincides with the boundary of such a religious congregation. For example, where the religious boundary is wider, the implictions are large in determining the structure of the jural community which relates the set of sovereignties. But the religious boundary does not define the political boundary. Similarly, a sovereignty may be endogamous or exogamous, may own territorial estate or not, and so on. These are crucial facts to know for comparative purposes, but they do not seem to identify the sovereignty.

[45] This is the man described in Chapter 5 to suggest a Cherokee personality type. The events are revealed almost exclusively by letters from the commander of the South Carolina garrison, Raymond Demere, to his superiors in Charles Town, and by his records of talks with Cherokees— in all, 24 reports (Jenkins 1949:October 13, 1756–August 26, 1757).

[46] I do not cite the many particular references in the Payne papers which are relevant; but see especially Payne MS, IVb:130–32 and 166–69.

[47] The records do not reveal how village councils and the tribal council were scheduled relative to one another and to the three major ceremonies. The presumption is strong that village councils were convened before and after a tribal council.

[48] Buttrick, in his loose handling of chronology, does not specify this organization as having emerged during Old Hop's time. To him, and to his informants as he reports them, this was the form of tribal government in the "old days," apparently stretching back forever. But this priestly structure for tribal councils did not exist in Moytoy's time, insofar as can be determined from the contemporary records. On the other hand, I have argued that the priestly structure did obtain in the villages from before 1730.

[49] There is some suggestion in the Payne manuscripts that in clan revenge the tribal priest chief had more than the usual village priest chief functions.

[50] Royce (1887) lists five cessions of land through 1775, and he does not include the cession just mentioned. There appear from contemporary records to have been seven altogether.

[51] This description must be used cautiously in the context of this study because, from internal evidence, Bartram appears often to have the Creek foremost in his mind. Bartram's visit did not occur until 1773, five years after the move of Great Warrior into the position of tribal chief, which I take to mark the arrival of the changes Bartram describes.

[52] I find only Bartram's statement as evidence for this new seating arrangement, which evidence is admittedly very thin. But a rearrangement of the seating strikes one as ingenious, and it fits so well with other known facts that I am inclined to believe that this occurred. The essential point, however, is the structural change. Bartram was one of the few observers who after 1767 did not report Great Warrior in the position of the tribal priest chief. He, probably erroneously, placed Little Carpenter in that role. Little Carpenter, it should be noted, had been the tribe's foremost emissary to foreign powers—a war role; so, whether Bartram is right or wrong as to who was chief, both possibilities support the suggestions as to the structural changes that had occurred.

[53] These thoughts have been expressed earlier in connection with a 1958 symposium on Cherokee-Iroquois studies (Gearing 1961).

[54] Nothing is known by me about primitive European political systems and the possible jural communities which related those sovereign units to one another.

[55] I have referred to the Cherokee state as voluntary, meaning by that that none of the units which joined exercised force on others of the units. This sense of voluntarism does not intend to preclude duress on all the units from some external source.

References Cited

ADAIR, JAMES
    1775   The history of the American Indians. London, E. and C. Dilly.
ADAMS, ROBERT M.
    1956   Some hypotheses on the development of early civilizations. American Antiquity, 21:227-32.
BARTRAM, WILLIAM
    1854   Observations on the Creek and Cherokee Indians. Transactions of the American Ethnological Society 3:11-81.
    1928   The travels of William Bartram. New York, Macy-Masius.
BENEDICT, RUTH
    1934   Patterns of culture. Boston, Houghton Mifflin Co.
BIRDWHISTELL, RAY L.
    1952   Introduction to kinesics—an annotation system for analysis of body motion and gesture. Louisville, Ky., University of Louisville.
BROWN, JOHN P.
    1938   Old frontiers. Kingsport, Tennessee, Southern Publishers, Inc.
CANDLER, ALLEN D., ed.
    1904-16   The colonial records of Georgia. Atlanta, The Franklin-Turner Co. and Charles P. Byrd, State Printer.
CLARK, WALTER, ed.
    1895-1905   The State records of North Carolina. Winston, M. J. and J. C. Steward, Printers to the State, and Goldsboro, Nash Brothers.
DRAKE, SAMUEL GARDNER
    1872   Early history of Georgia. Boston, D. Clapp and Son.
EASTON, DAVID
    1959   Political anthropology. In Biennial review of anthropology, Bernard Siegel, ed. Stanford, Stanford University Press.
ELLIS, FLORENCE HAWLEY
    1951   Patterns of aggression and the war cult in southwestern Pueblos. Southwestern Journal of Anthropology 7:177-201.
EVANS-PRITCHARD, E. E.
    1940   The Nuer. Clarendon Press, Oxford.
FIRTH, RAYMOND
    1954   Social organization and social change. Journal of the Royal Anthropological Institute of Great Britain and Ireland 84:1-20.
FORTES, MEYER
    1940   The political system of the Tallensi in the Northern territories of the Gold Coast. In African political systems, M. Fortes and E. E. Evans-Pritchard. London, Oxford University Press.
    1945   The dynamics of clanship among the Tallensi. London, Oxford University Press.
FORTES, MEYER AND E. E. EVANS-PRITCHARD, eds.
    1940   African political systems. London, Oxford University Press.
GEARING, FRED
    1958   The structural poses of 18th century Cherokee villages. American Anthropologist 60:1148-57.
    1961   The rise of the Cherokee state as an instance in a class: the "Mesopotamian" career to statehood. Bureau of American Ethnology Bulletin 180:125-34.

119

GILBERT, WILLIAM HARLEM, JR.
  1943 The Eastern Cherokee. Bureau of American Ethnology Bulletin 133.
  1955 Eastern Cherokee social organization. *In* Social anthropology of North American tribes, Fred Eggan, ed. Chicago, University of Chicago Press.
GOFFMAN, ERVING
  1959 The presentation of self in everyday life. New York, Doubleday and Co., Inc.
GRANT, LUDOVIC
  1909 Relations of facts. South Carolina Historical and Genealogical Magazine 10:54–68.
GULICK, JOHN
  1958 Problems of cultural communication—the Eastern Cherokees. The American Indian 8:20–31.
  1959 The self-corrective circuit and trait persistence in conservative Eastern Cherokee culture. *In* Research Previews, Vol. 6, No. 3.
HAYWOOD, JOHN
  1823 Natural and aboriginal history of Tennessee. Nashville, George Wilson.
JACOBSEN, THORKILD
  1943 Primitive democracy in ancient Mesopotamia. Journal of Near Eastern Studies. 2:(3:)159–72.
JENKINS, WILLIAM SUMNER, ed.
  1949 Records of the states of the United States, a microfilm compilation. S.C.M. 1a, 2 reels. Washington, Library of Congress Photoduplication Service.
LEACH, EDMUND R.
  1954 Political systems of highland Burma. Cambridge, Harvard University Press.
LLEWELLYN, K. N., AND E. A. HOEBEL
  1941 The Cheyenne way. Norman, University of Oklahoma Press.
LOGAN, JOHN H.
  1859 A history of the upper country of South Carolina, from the earliest periods to the close of the War of Independence. Vol. I. Charleston, S. G., Courtenay and Co.
MIDDLETON, J. AND D. TAIT
  1958 Tribes without rulers: studies in African segmentary systems. London, Routledge and Kegan Paul.
MILLER, WALTER
  1960 Authority and collective action in Fox society. *In* Documentary history of the Fox project, Fred Gearing, Robert McC. Netting, and Lisa R. Peattie, eds. Chicago, University of Chicago Press.
MILLING, CHAPMAN J., ed.
  1940 Red Carolinians. Chapel Hill, University of North Carolina Press.
  1951 Colonial South Carolina: two contemporary descriptions. Columbia, University of South Carolina Press.
MOONEY, JAMES
  1891 Sacred formulas of the Cherokees. Bureau of American Ethnology Bulletin 7 (1885–86).
  1900 Myths of the Cherokees. Bureau of American Ethnology 19th Annual Report, Pt. 1. Washington, Government Printing Office.
NADEL, S. F.
  1951 Foundations of social anthropology. Glencoe, Ill., The Free Press.
PAYNE, JOHN HOWARD
  MS The Payne-Buttrick papers. Books I, II, III, IVa, IVb. Chicago, Ayer Collection, Newberry Library.
READ, K. E.
  1959 Leadership and consensus in New Guinea society. American Anthropologist 61:425–36.

REDFIELD, ROBERT
  1953 The primitive world and its transformations. Ithaca, N. Y., Cornell University Press.
  1955 The little community: viewpoints for the study of a human whole. Chicago, University of Chicago Press.
RIESMAN, DAVID
  1950 The lonely crowd. New Haven, Yale University Press.
ROYCE, CHARLES C.
  1887 The Cherokee nation of Indians. Bureau of American Ethnology 5th Annual Report. Washington, Government Printing Office.
SALLEY, A. S., JR., ed.
  1907 Journals of the Commons House of Assembly of South Carolina for the four sessions of 1693. Columbia, The State Company.
  1930 Journal of the proceedings of the Honorable, the Governor, and Council, May 29, 1721–June 10, 1721. Atlanta, Foote and Davies Company.
  1945 Journal of the Commons House of Assembly of South Carolina, November 1, 1725–April 30, 1726. Joint Committee on Printing, General Assembly of South Carolina.
SAUNDERS, WILLIAM L., ed.
  1886–90 The colonial records of North Carolina. Raleigh, Josephus Daniels, Printer to the State.
SCHOOLCRAFT, HENRY R.
  1860 Historical and statistical information respecting the history, condition and prospects of the Indian tribes of the United States. Philadelphia, 1851–68, Lippincott, Grambo.
THOMAS, ROBERT K.
  1958 Cherokee values and world view. Unpublished MS., University of North Carolina.
TITIEV, MISCHA
  1944 Old Oraibi, a study of the Hopi Indians of the third mesa. Cambridge, Mass. Papers of the Peabody Museum of Archaeology and Ethnology, Vol. 22, No. 1.
WEBER, MABEL L.
  1918 An Indian land grant in 1734. The South Carolina Historical and Genealogical Magazine 19:157–61.
WILLIAMS, SAMUEL COLE
  1927 (ed.) Lieutenant Henry Timberlake's memoirs, 1756–1765. Johnson City, Tennessee, The Watauga Press.
  1928 (ed.) Early travels in the Tennessee country, 1540–1800. Johnson City, Tennessee, The Watauga Press.
  1937 Dawn of Tennessee Valley and Tennessee history. Johnson City, Tennessee, The Watauga Press.
WILLIS, WILLIAM SHEDRICK
  1955 Colonial conflict and the Cherokee Indians, 1710–1760. Unpublished Ph.D. thesis, Columbia University.

Index

122